Mary
in Scripture,
Liturgy, and the
Catholic Tradition

RENÉ LAURENTIN

Paulist Press
New York / Mahwah, NJ

Cover Image by Luril Kuzo / Dreamstime.com
Cover and book design by Lynn Else

Library of Congress Control Number: 2014953576

ISBN 978-0-8091-4808-0 (paperback)

Published by Paulist Press
997 Macarthur Boulevard
Mahwah, New Jersey 07430

www.paulistpress.com

Printed and bound in the
United States of America

CONTENTS

INTRODUCTION

WHY WRITE THIS BOOK?

Good question. Why have I been attracted to and fasci-
nated by Mary's presence for so many decades?

Mary's presence is the presence of the first of all creatures; she is above the angels, not by nature or stature, but
through the greatest love that can abide in a simple creature, in the radiance of divine love. True, God alone is love,
but she was the most beloved of creatures, the one who
was the most responsive, the one who most loved God and
who gave human birth to the person of the Son of God.
She was the sole human cause of his divine presence on
earth.

Her presence, therefore, is not an imposing presence
that is searing or thundering, but a discreet and modest
presence that is without ostentation. The most glorious of
creatures is also the most humble. She is the greatest
because she was the smallest, Péguy says, paraphrasing
the *Magnificat* of Mary herself:

> The Lord has looked on the poverty of his servant,
> He has done great things for me.

She was well aware of this contrast.

Hers was not a presence in and of itself. There is no
such thing as a presence in and of itself. Anyone who is in
and of himself or herself through egoism or narcissism is
not a presence: his or her egocentrism closes in upon

itself. But God is not closed in upon himself; he is open. The Father gives himself eternally to the Son and the Son gives himself in return. Their mutual gift, their love itself, is deep within them; it is the Holy Spirit. Lastly, the Father, who alone exists in himself, does not exist for himself, but for the Son and the Spirit, and through the Son and the Spirit. He creates worlds, among which we can know the cosmos (and the minuscule grain of dust that is planet Earth, our "vast world," which is part of the observable cosmos fourteen billion light years across).

God is open to other beings. He is all. There is nothing without him, and he creates other beings out of nothing. His is a communicative presence.

Mary is not God. She is a pure creature who owes her whole existence and all of her beauty to God and who renders them to God out of incomparable love. Mary, therefore, is present in God, through God, and for God but also for other creatures, for us. Her primary presence is in God: she is for God and for others, because she embodies his supreme love in creation.

But she embodies that supreme love in the person of Christ—God who is made man in her. He owes everything to her, in human terms; the child Jesus knew how to savor her presence. But Mary also knew how to savor the presence of God, as she sings so joyfully in her *Magnificat*:

> My soul magnifies the Lord,
> And my spirit rejoices in God my savior…
> Holy is his name.

Her presence is first of all that of a mother: the mother of God in humanity, the mother of us all, in him and through him, as we shall see.

The mother is the supreme presence here below—the first face, the first enveloping and communicative smile, to awaken the baby Jesus to his humanity.

THE ORIGINS OF STUDY

Ever since I was a young man at the seminary, I always wanted to seek out the best; I was always captivated by words and texts that evoked the presence of Mary: it was like an invitation to go deeper, to discover more.

I assembled a first anthology, then I dated the most revealing texts.

In the sixties, using a method that allowed me to penetrate deeper and to address many issues, I drew up a chronological file and formatted it, using the method that has often allowed me to do an in-depth study of a subject, using historical, traditional, diachronic, and synchronic means, and the profound life and mind of the Church that enlivens the centuries.

I was working to complete the book when I noticed that Stefano de Fiores, the most celebrated of the Italian Mariologists, was directing a priest's doctoral thesis on this very subject and with the very same title. It would have been indiscreet and risky to go ahead. When his book was published, it proved worthy of the subject; we communicated with each other a few times with the aim of working together. He got back to me later, but I was the one who was busy at the time.

Once or twice I went back to the file, but without ever completing it. Then failing eyesight prevented me, for a while, from finishing it. I began it again with Patrick Sbalchiero, after my *Dictionary of "Apparitions."* We completed it together, and that same complementarity saved all my efforts from coming to naught.

After having worked alone, I came to gradually learn the value of teamwork and collaboration, which will increasingly be the way of the future.

THE WORD

Presence is a simple word: to be present is to be there, today, in reality. *Presence* rhymes with *absence*, for philological reasons that we will see presently. To be there or not be there. Presence is a fundamental fact of daily experience. A psychologist once said to me, "For me there are two kinds of people, those who are there and those who are not there."

It is true; there are insignificant people whose existence does not really emerge fully. We cannot even see them. Others exist for those around them. *Presence* means a lot more for an actor, far more than simply his or her technique or talent. It is presence that makes him or her succeed. It is the deciding factor of great careers. The comedian arrives and seems to fill the screen. We cannot forget him. The public needs to see him again, from Charlie Chaplin first and foremost, to the French stars Maurice Chevalier, Raimu, and Gabin. I am naming men here rather than women, because for women, the exploitation of the erotic factor tends often to interfere with the idea of presence (hence, the varying degrees of ambiguity surrounding Marlene Dietrich, Marilyn Monroe, and even more so, Brigitte Bardot). But the phenomenon of presence is much clearer with older women such as Marguerite Moreno or Simone Signoret. Here we have the presence of an actor whose function is to lend verisimilitude to life and fiction. However, this is not the context in which we wish to speak of the presence of Mary.

Etymologically, *absence* and *presence* are formed by the root of the verb to be (*ens*) with two different prefixes:

ab (the prefix of the word *ab-sence*) means
  "a disjunction: not being there."
pre (the prefix of the word *pre-sence*) means,
  by contrast, "what is before (*prae*) one's eyes, that
  which is offered to our grasp: that which is close to us."

Presence and absence direct us to an existence that counts. In one case, it is accessible; in the other it is not. Like all opposites, the two words are then closer to each other than they seem; as Aristotle says, "Opposites are in the same category."

To speak of absence is to express a lack, a privation, a frustration; although many absences can signify total indifference. But if we can speak about it, it must exist.

Language contains all instinctive philosophy—that is, what man has invested in creating language—here, we are speaking of a philosophy of communion. In grammatical terms, the present designates the time period of verbs that express not the past, or the future, or the abstraction of the infinitive, but what is current. The present has such impact and prestige that, nowadays, writers prefer to use the present rather than the past. So much so that in French the perfect (which was for a long time the most-used tense) is falling out of use and seems to be disappearing.

Regarding Mary, we must understand that this character from the past (at the time of Herod and the emperor Augustus, whose presence imposed itself on their time but no longer does today) does not belong to that past time, but is right here. But in what way?

To say that she is present is to say that she exists today, and that she exercises an influence that can be identified, recognized, and known, and that is accessible through experience.

It is not an easy subject. It has its pitfalls, such as emotionalism, autosuggestion, artificial or uncontrolled mysticism, and so on. In order to avoid these pitfalls, we will not begin with mystical testimonies. We will first of all pursue the issue on the level of the fundamental gifts of the Church's life by looking at various overlapping aspects, where the overlap will be useful in thoroughly examining the issue. These aspects include, first, Mary's presence in the life of Christ, as attested to by Scripture; second, her presence in the liturgy (*lex orandi*), where the Church expresses its life; and third, Mary's presence in community life; that is, the local and universal Churches. Only after that will we present and elucidate witnesses who have experienced Mary's presence throughout the history of the Church. We can then respond, by way of conclusion, to the following questions:

- What is Mary's presence in revelation and in Christian tradition? What is her importance and character? How can we distinguish her presence from God's presence?
- How can we explain it and where can we find it? How does it emerge from the current role of Mary in the Church?
- How can we discern, live, and cultivate that presence, without being subjective, and without giving it either too much emphasis or too little within the communion of saints?

HISTORICAL OVERVIEW

In Scripture, Mary appears from the outset as virgin and mother of the Messiah, the Son of God (Luke 1:2; Matt 1:2), closely linked to the life of Christ and the birth of the Church at Pentecost (Acts 1:14; cf John 2:1–12; 19:25–27; Rev 12). At the Council of Ephesus (431), she was proclaimed "Mother of God" (*Theotokos*).

In the seventeenth century, in reaction against the Protestant reforms (1515), the Marian movement began. It gave significant development to the Catholic faith, since the Council of Trent (1545–63) had not then judged it useful to produce any documents on the Virgin when it published all the others. Opposition was not so determined at the outset. After the French Revolution in 1789, the movement began again. And the nineteenth century was marked by the definition of the immaculate conception by Pius IX (December 8, 1854) and then in the twentieth century by the definition of the assumption by Pius XII (1950).

For a long time, the Marian movement continued in a living, intimate, spiritual way, without any need for dogmatic or legal definition. Since the late nineteenth century the movement has tried to promulgate a definition of Mary as the universal "mediatrix" of all grace (Pius XII deliberately waived the objections of the committee created by the Holy Office). Is Mary mediatrix of the graces of the Old Testament and is she an intermediary for sanctifying grace because she is the actualization of divine life in the Church and in every Christian, through the *immediate* action of the Holy Spirit? The Holy See has not made other attempts because the Virgin has little need of official declarations; the important thing is that she becomes better known and loved, whether by doctrinal means or through our link with her as our mother.

The bishops had many requests during the preparation for Vatican II: two hundred of them asked that Mary be defined as "mediatrix, coredemptrix, and queen." During the council, the Polish Cardinal Wyszynski and several other bishops of different nationalities asked for a definition of the "spiritual motherhood" of Mary.

In the 1990s, Misvalle launched a new petition aimed at defining Mary as "co-redeemer, mediatrix and advocate," on the basis of the private revelations of Ida Peerdman (apparitions in Amsterdam that have now been recognized). This approach was not successful, given the difficulties posed by the Congregation for the Doctrine of the Faith and the Unity of Christians, respectively. Still other titles were added to these five that were put forward for an official definition, including *auxiliatrix* and *adjutrix* (mentioned by the Vatican in *Lumen Gentium* 8, in the passage that explains how Mary's mediating in Christ in no way detracts from his unique title of Mediator [Titus 2:5]).

Seven titles represent the different but related ways of addressing Mary, under which we try to define her actual function in the Church and the diversity of her roles. Tradition also throws up other titles similar to *coredemptrix* and the like; titles such as *salvatrix* and *redemptrix* that arose in the seventeenth century, but have been found wanting.

But these attempts at explaining the organic and unitary function of Mary in the work of salvation did not clarify the debate. The great movement launched in 1913 by Cardinal Mercier in an attempt to put the definition of the mediation of Mary on a solid footing tended toward coredemption, not without objections from many theologians, and not only Protestants (Goossens and others).

After careful consideration, it seems to us that theological research in this immense area regarding Mary's participation in salvation must become less of a cause for petitionary action. These petitions were signed by people of good will who were presented with the petition as they were coming out of Mass, with the phrase "sign this petition for the glory of Mary" without always understanding either the issue or its meaning. It was, if you like, a false good idea, or even a deadlock. The important thing is to engage in thoroughgoing theological work that can be used to solve this lively but confused doctrinal question.

This theological enquiry, like all others, must be pursued not in abstraction, which only complicates matters, but with a permanent link to spiritual life and personal experience, which are the indispensable elements required in order to arrive at an authentic contemplative theology that is well founded in Scripture and Tradition. This approach also enlivens the faith and gives Mary her true place in the life of the Church and in ecumenism. For over half a century, this is what attracted me to the *Presence of Mary*, which she lived out within herself, but also expressed, I discovered, earlier and earlier.

This word *presence* is a more satisfactory expression than the other seven titles mentioned above, which have tended to excessively polarize matters while each has its own ambiguities: *coredemptrix* seems to put Christ and the Virgin Mary on the same level; *mediatrix* makes us forget that Christ is the only mediator between God and humankind; *advocate* makes us forget that the Advocate (Greek: *paracletos*; Latin: *advocatus*) is the biblical title for the Holy Spirit, and so on.

This is why I never stopped pursuing conceptual and crucial research, both theologically and spiritually, as a source and theme that go far beyond the word *presence*. Presence is a tangible fact, rather than simply a concept. But this concept regarding Mary in her relationship with the people of God makes her the closest of all because she is the closest and most united to God in Jesus Christ. This is what I have tried to bring to light, not so much in order to develop a doctrinal concept, but to clarify, vivify, and deepen our connection with Mary.

I
THE PRESENCE OF MARY IN SCRIPTURE

Before we begin studying the presence of Mary on the doctrinal and spiritual level, before defining her, studying her, and deepening our knowledge, we need to examine who she is in the context of history, because nothing else on earth has such historical origins—not even the revelation that God has given to his people and that drew them little by little into personal and communal knowledge of him. Elsewhere we find the specificity itself, the meaning and the human dimension of Christianity, coming out of the revelation to the people of God, that Jesus Christ himself entered completely the transcendent principle of a new covenant, which is not a break with what went before but its renewal and accomplishment, according to the words of Christ: "I came not to abolish the law, but to complete it" (Matt 5:17).

We will therefore review this presence of Mary in the first revelation: to Abraham and Moses, to the prophets and sages of Israel; then in Christ, the founder and very principle of the Church; then in the Church from different angles after the completion of this revelation. We must evaluate Mary's presence by considering opinions that are sometimes extreme and contradictory.

ALL SCRIPTURE CONCERNS MARY

So said Pseudo-Bernard in the twelfth century.[1] He meant this in the sense that typology, symbolism, and mysticism extend the literal meaning indefinitely.

On the other hand, Catholics and Protestants in the sixteenth century began tacitly to agree when speaking of the silence of Scripture on the Virgin Mary. The Catholics, whose curiosity and appetite to know everything was not satisfied by Scripture, turned instead to the Apocrypha and their traditions, deductions, and inventions on the margins of Scripture. Protestants, bristling with the excesses of those times, steeped themselves gradually in suppression and hostility. This distance toward Scripture considerably aggravated the dispute. In the last few decades, the main benefit of ecumenism is that Catholics have been able to find the Virgin Mary *in* Scripture, while Protestants have rediscovered her *through* Scripture.

THE OLD TESTAMENT

Does the Old Testament speak of Mary? Tradition has recognized three ways of answering this question: historical, prophetic, and typological anticipation of her presence.

HISTORICAL ANTICIPATION

Mary was prepared through the history of the people into which she was born. She owes them her birth and her upbringing. This is not insignificant for any human being, and it helps us to understand her through not only her historical but also her biblical roots. It is in this way that Mary was anticipated prophetically and typologically by the Old Testament: the prophets announce her in words (*sensus verborum*) and typology announces her in reality (*sensus rerum*) in the typological sense.

2

This perfection of holiness, of faith, of acceptance is only possible after a lengthy preparation. In the *Magnificat* itself, Mary's faith (Luke 1:45–47) is like Abraham's faith. In some ways, it is its completion and fulfillment.

PROPHETIC PROCLAMATIONS

There are three Old Testament prophecies that explicitly announce the Mother of the Messiah:

1. Isaiah 7:14: "Look, the young woman is with child and shall bear a son, and shall name him Immanuel." Matthew confirms the virginal and eschatological nature of this prophecy already explained by the Greek Septuagint (second century BC): "'Look, the virgin shall conceive and bear a son, / and they shall name him / Emmanuel,' which means, 'God is with us'" (Matt 1:23). (The prophet Isaiah quotes the prophecy addressed to King David in 2 Samuel 7:14, where the role of the mother is not mentioned.)
2. Micah 5:2–3 reinforces the importance of the mother: "But you, O Bethlehem...from you shall come forth for me one who is to rule in Israel...up until the time when she who is in labor has brought forth." The end of the prophecy gives new importance to the mother. This is what Matthew confirms in 2:1–4.
3. Genesis 3:15 is recognized as the most significant prediction about Mary: after original sin, God punishes the tempter (the serpent), telling it that a descendant of the woman, that is, Christ, will fight against it, according to the prophecy. The Virgin does not have the predominant role that is attributed to her by the Latin Vulgate translation by Saint Jerome in the fourth century. That translation says: "She shall crush your head," but grammatically and linguistically the correct translation is "He will strike your head, and you will strike his heel," because it is the same verb *shouf* (which is found four times in the Bible) that expresses this mutual enmity without specifying who will strike the serpent.

What justifies the traditional messianic interpretation is that the prophecy has a dynastic quality to it and involves the image of the mother in a battle in which victory is assured.

TYPOLOGICAL PREPARATIONS

The birth of Jesus Christ (in his genealogy according to Matt 1:1–18) through Mary is preceded by four women who were prostitutes or adulteresses and who played a significant role in the dynastic succession: Tamar, Rahab, Ruth, and "Uriah's wife." Mary represents a break in this genealogy in which it is the fathers who beget the children (this occurs forty-two times in the genealogy). When we come to the last link in the chain, it is not Joseph who begets Jesus; the begetting that we expect is replaced by "Joseph the husband of Mary, of whom Jesus was born, who is called the Messiah" (1:16).

Verse 18 stipulates that Jesus is from the Holy Spirit (from the Greek *ek-*). Similarly, Luke corrects his first conviction with the phrase "as was thought" (Luke 3:23), saying only that "Jesus…was the son (as was thought) of Joseph"; this is far-reaching.[2] In Luke, Mary is both the eschatological Daughter of Zion in which the Son of God is personally conceived as man, and also the new ark of the covenant (Exod 40:34–35) in which God comes to reside personally and physically.

The New Testament also draws together two lines that could appear heterogeneous and contradictory in an unexpected way: on the one hand, the promise of a Messiah, son of David; on the other hand, the promise that God himself will come to reside among his people and establish himself as king. These are the two promises that come together and are brought about in Mary.

This coming together is called the incarnation (as explained in John 1:13); Luke describes this mystery in a fuller and more tangible way through Mary's experience.

He identifies this woman's child as the Son of God. Thus he attributes to him a remarkable collection of exalted titles: "Great" (without restriction or relativism), "Holy" (Luke 1:35), "Lord" (1:43; 2:11), "Savior" (2:11) and "Salvation" (2:30; cf. 1:68), "Glory" (2:32; cf. 1:35), and "Light" (2:32), which are given to him throughout Luke 1—2.[3]

Symbolically, God creates the woman without sin (immaculate) in Eve, the mother of all the living, who turned away from God, and God takes up his plan for the woman through the mothers that the Bible often honors in genealogies: notably Sarah, Rachel, Ruth (whose initiative was prominent in the dynastic genealogy of the Messiah), and all the heroines, real or symbolic, whom the Bible holds up to us, including Judith, Esther, and others.

In short, Mary, the principle of the new creation announced by the prophets, appears both as virgin, immaculate, and mother of all the living, like the figure of Eve, and as "blessed among women" like Leah, for having given birth to the fathers of ten of the tribes of Israel, especially to Judah, the father of the dynastic branch. There is no need for us to recapitulate further the typology of Mary and its significant stages throughout the Bible according to the plan of God, who is the supreme author of history. It is not the details that count, but rather God's intention, his plan that unfolds gradually, through the vicissitudes of freedom and the sins of humanity.

The prototype of Mary is not so much the mothers who have given birth to men time after time throughout the generations, but, more spiritually and more deeply, the "Daughter of Zion." This phrase symbolizes the people of God at its best—the faithful people, and above all the obscure and humble people in whom the eschatological achievement came to fruition—it was ultimately Mary who came at the end of that hidden line. She was the mother not of a new and indefinite series of generations, but of the Messiah, Son of God, born without sin, who neither married nor fathered anyone, because in him all of humanity is summed up: one vine, says Jesus (John 15); one body (humankind saved by him), writes Saint Paul. Catholic and ecumenical exegesis of the twentieth century understood that Mary was chosen and named after the eschatological Daughter of Zion. In her, this symbolic personalization becomes real and personal. How wonderful it is that she responded to God in the name of all of humanity, in agreeing, despite enormous risks, to become the mother of the Messiah, Son of God, in whom everything will be made new! The same message of the annunciation given by Mary tells of two, if not three, tremendous predictions.

When God eventually comes into her (*bequirbek*: literally, "into your innards"; cf. Zeph 3:14–17), there are three other prophecies all beginning with the words repeated by the archangel Gabriel addressing Mary:

> Rejoice [Daughter of Zion]: the Lord is with you…You will conceive and give birth to [Greek: *engastri*, as in gastric] the Son of the Most High. (Luke 1:28–32)[4]

The Second Vatican Council (*Lumen Gentium* 55) authoritatively confirms this typological identification of Mary with the Daughter of Zion.

But the Daughter of Zion is also the mother of the new people, the people of the promise, as we see in Isaiah 66, and this is taken up again in Revelation 12, where the mother of the Messiah—the male infant who will reign over the nations—is also the mother of the people saved by Christ, and she helps him in his battle against the dragon—Satan, who pursues the Church after having pursued Mary (last verse of Rev 12). This typology is therefore very profound and very coherent. God's plan is summarized both in the annunciation message (Luke 1:26–38) and in biblical eschatology (Rev 12; cf. Rev 21):

Zephaniah 3:15–17

Sing aloud, O daughter Zion;
   shout, O Irsael!
Rejoice and exult with
   all your heart,
O daughter Jerusalem!
The king of Israel, *the* LORD,
is in your midst;
Do not fear, O Zion…
The LORD, your God,
Is in your midst, a warrior
   who gives victory;

Luke 1:28–33

Daughter of Zion

"Rejoice,

favored one!
The Lord is with you."

"Do not be afraid, Mary…
And now, you will conceive
in your womb
And bear a son,
He will be called the Son of
   the Most High.
He will reign over the
   house of Jacob
forever, and of his kingdom
   there will be no end."

In the passage about the annunciation, Mary is identified not just as the Daughter of Zion (a symbol that she embodies and makes real) but as the ark of the covenant. Mary typologically makes real the prophecy made to the Daughter of Zion, of God coming to live within her, like a new ark of the covenant:[5]

Exodus 40:34

Then the cloud

[*episkiasen*]
covered
the tent of meeting,
and the glory of the LORD
filled the tabernacle.

Luke 1:35

…the power of the Most
   High will
overshadow
you;
therefore
the child to be born…
will be called Son of God.

In Luke 1:35 (which encapsulates the message), the angel responds to Mary, who then questions this because she is a virgin and thus cannot be the mother of the Messiah. The angel then confirms his message: everything about this virgin birth will be the work of God, just as everything was of God when he first appeared among his people, in the ark of the covenant. His presence in the vessel constructed by Moses will not be simply a figure of speech, but the true procreation of the Son of God, and Mary will herself be the Daughter of Zion:

The child to be born...will be called Son of God.

The eternal child of the Father becomes the human child of Mary, both Son of God and Son of the woman who is blessed among women.

The *Magnificat* confirms this typology: the action of grace passes from the person of Mary, the Lord's humble servant (Luke 1:46–48), to the whole of God's humble people, then to its original personalization in Abraham. The *Magnificat* ends with him as it began with Mary (Luke 1:55); it is the ultimate fulfillment that shows the depth of her faith.

Some Scripture scholars also posit that Luke 2:35 refers back to Ezekiel 14:17:

Ezek 14:17	**Luke 2:35**
Let a sword	a sword
Pass through the land	will pierce your own soul
(i.e., Israel).	too.

In short, Mary is the ultimate realization of the people of God, the mother of the Messiah, and the ultimate fulfillment of God's coming among his people, of which she becomes a member par excellence and its eschatological fulfillment.

In other words, God, who takes up residence in the ark of wood, teaches Mary that he will come to reside in her like a new and living ark of the covenant. Luke shows this typology also in the passage about the visitation, which, with a wealth of detail, repeats the phrases in 2 Samuel 6:1–11. The passage on the visitation, in a significant way, parallels literally the passage about the ark of the covenant being transferred to the country of Judah, to Jerusalem:[6]

2 Samuel 6:1–2	**Luke 1:39**
David...set out and went from Baale-judah, to bring up from there	Mary set out and went with haste to a Judean town in the hill country
the ark of God	*Identified as Mary*

They both exclaim in a similar way:

The utterance of David (2 Sam 6:9) "How can the ark of the LORD come into my care?"	*The utterance of Elizabeth (Luke 1:43)* "And why has this happened to me, that the mother of my Lord come to me?"

And at the end of the visitation passage:

2 Samuel 6:11	**Luke 1:56**
The ark of the LORD remained in the house of Obed-edom the Gittite *three months*	And Mary remained with her about *three months*

Typological exegesis down the centuries has multiplied types and symbols, and this has resulted in a proliferation of gratuitous and unverifiable parallels in the text.

However, we need to concentrate on what is based on the Bible itself, the Word of God.

CONCLUSION

Mary is certainly present in the Old Testament, but implicitly, by anticipation, and discernable only retrospectively. She is prepared; she is a part of God's plan (typology) and his promises (prophecies); she is God's masterpiece; she is a re-creation of the first woman, Eve, and is created by the hands of God (Gen 2) without stain; she also parallels the patriarch Abraham as the perfection of his faith. In her, God brings about his coming, thereby giving meaning to everything that preceded it. The word *presence*, therefore, does have meaning in this context, but it is by analogy and in a limited sense. It is in the New Testament that this presence becomes explicit and manifest, and takes on a magnitude that we do not see with any other character from the New Testament.

THE NEW TESTAMENT

From start to finish, Mary's presence in the New Testament is pervasive: from the incarnation (John 1:13; Luke 1—2; cf. Gal 4:4) to the public ministry of Jesus (John 2:12); his death (John 19:25–27), the ascension, and Pentecost, at the beginnings of the Church (Acts 1:14); and lastly, through the end of time (Rev 12:1–17).

In all these stages, what comes to the fore is Mary's mission as mother and woman and her faith and supreme holiness, particularly in Luke 1—2 and in the writings of John. It is not our intention here to outline the chronology of the texts, nor to recall the references to Mary during the public life of Jesus where her role is minimal. Instead, we must evaluate the importance of her presence: how it relates to the structure of the New Testament, its role in the incarnation, its paramount importance, its typology, and its spiritual radiance.

But our objective is not to uncover historical detail, which is already difficult to date, since we are ignorant of the written or oral tradition prior to the Gospels, and even of its exact date. What is important with regard to Mary's presence is the structure and the meaning of the New Testament texts.

First, a material and uncontested historical fact: Jesus has a "mother" (there are twenty references to this in the New Testament: Matthew 1:18; 2:13, 14, 20; Mark 3:32; Luke 1:43; 2:33, 34, 48, 51; 8:20; John 2:1, 3, 5, 12; 19:25–27; and Acts 1:14); and she is called "Mary" (Hebrew: *Myriam*). Her name is mentioned twenty-three times: Matthew 1:16, 18, 20; 2:11; 13:5 (five times); Mark 6:3 (once); Luke 1:25—2:34 (twelve times); and Acts 1:14 (once). But John (like Paul) uses the name "mother of Jesus." "The mother" and "the disciple" are the two great anonymous figures in the fourth Gospel.

If we only had this fact, it would be difficult to give a value to it, because Christ's words in the Synoptic Gospels run counter to the thesis, which is typical of the Mariology of the Counter-Reformation, according to which divine motherhood is higher than grace—because, paradoxically, Mariologists said that the Gospel texts in Mark 3:31–33 and Luke 11:5–7 were "anti-mariological."

Texts in which Jesus contrasts family and kingdom as flesh and spirit seem to have arisen to counter the dynastic tendency in which two cousins of Jesus had been chosen as the first two bishops of the primitive community of Jerusalem. The evangelists were particularly careful to show that a family connection was not, for Jesus himself, a claim to fame; Christ's relations in the kingdom are based on hearing the Word and putting it into practice. But, in Mary's case, she was the prime and perfect exemplar of that. But neither the Gospels (not Paul, nor Matt 1—

2) say it formally, although Luke 1:28 and 56 express Mary's privileged relationship with the Holy Spirit; and John does not say it explicitly, although he ascribes to her the role of a sign, an act of intercession (John 2:4), and a maternal role with regard to Christ and the disciples.

So we hesitate to interpret the scope of these texts (Matthew and John), and we could then ask, as R.E. Brown did, whether they are symbolic or historical. We also have Luke's testimony with regard to Mary's vocation, where her faith and charisms seem to be a foretaste of Pentecost. This is why we basically need to stop at Luke 1—2, which explains the meaning of Mary's relationship not just to Christ, but to the Holy Spirit, which is a theological and charismatic relationship. This fact allows us to know the profound importance of the texts in John that show Mary's functional and symbolic dimensions without explaining her deep theological life, which was already shown in Luke 1—2. John refers to that text, since he was already aware of it. The theme of Mary's presence would have no meaning without knowledge of the theological and charismatic life that is its starting point and is a type and model of the Church and Christians.

LUKE 1—2

Unlike Matthew, Luke considers Mary not as an object, but as an active subject. When we compare Matthew with Luke, we find that the positions of Joseph and Mary are reversed, from their own perspectives. Semiotically, according to Matthew 1—2, it is Joseph who is the hero of the infancy narrative, in which everything is orchestrated by God. In Luke, it is Mary. Luke locates her at Nazareth and Matthew is silent on the matter. Matthew explains the value of Joseph the "just"; Luke, that of Mary. Luke puts forward two essential points:

The annunciation has long been thought to fit under the literary genre of "birth narratives" (sometimes going so far as to ignore the powerful originality of the text in order to make it fit that prefabricated category). But recent authors have instead admitted that the annunciation is, more accurately, a passage about a "calling." The nearest model for this is the calling of Gideon—just as Gideon receives from on high the name "mighty warrior" (Judg 6:12), so Mary receives the name *Kekaritomê* (Luke 1:28). But even here, the annunciation shows differences when compared to other vocation passages. Her name, *Kekaritomê*, does not signify a function (not even the function of mother), but rather the grace of God, which puts her at a much more exalted level. In this sense, the annunciation transcends the literary genre found in Judges 6. Afterward, Mary receives her mission as mother, but it is again in a new and unexpected way. She is not exalted like the glorious *guébirah* of the Son of David (Luke 1:32b–33; Isa 7:14). First of all she is told that she will be the mother of the Son of God (Luke 1:32a). It is after this that Jesus is identified as the "Son of David," without which Luke would struggle to convey to us just how he could be linked to David, not being Joseph's son (Luke 34, etc.). The only explanation for this is topographical: Jesus is born in the "city of David" (Luke 2:4, 11).

Mary's mission is explained above all as the dissemination of the Holy Spirit that first came upon her (Luke 1:35) and which extends to John the Baptist (Luke 1:15) and Elizabeth (Luke 1:41) when Mary visits her cousin. Her presence within the Mystery of Salvation is not simply based on her role as mother through the conception and gestation of the Messiah, but on her living link with the Holy Spirit that comes "upon" her (Luke 1:35).

She is not simply a means or instrument of God's action in order to give birth to the Son of God. She is, first of all, loved by God. This is what the new name she has been given means: *Kekaritomenê*, "object of God's favor, full of grace" (1:28). The verb *charitoô* means essentially

"God's benevolence" and not created grace, but verbs ending in *oô* signify a transformation of being: *leuchoô* means "to bleach"; *chrysoô*, "to gild"; *kakoô*, "to damage"; *douloô*, "to enslave"; and so on. So Mary is transformed by kindness, love, and God's grace. To prevent any doubt about the meaning of this new name, the messenger then makes this statement: "You have found favor with God" (1:30). Mary, then, is chosen freely by the love of God, before she even receives her role as mother. And that is not without importance.

The love of God does not smother her in a possessive and reductive way. It is directed toward her as a free and conscious person. Luke 1 makes this clear. Mary actively pondered in her heart (*dialogizeto*, 1:29), in contrast to Zechariah on whom "fear fell" passively. Mary's question was not an objection (Luke 1:34): "How can this be, since I am a virgin?" And unlike the priest Zechariah, she has the right to speak and the right to a response, which reveals the depths of the mystery (in contrast with the punishment inflicted on Zechariah). Her freedom remains profound, according to the grace she received. She declares herself to be "the handmaid of the Lord" (Luke 1:38, 48). She leaves "in haste" and goes adventurously across the mountains, driven by the momentum of the gift of the Spirit (like the missionaries of the early Church in Acts 5:10; 8:26–27, 36; 9:15; 10:20; 16:7, and more, where the word *poreuomai* is used as in Acts 1:39). Elizabeth recognizes that Mary's true happiness and her true value is her faith: "And blessed is she who believed that there would be a fulfillment of what was spoken to her by the Lord." (Luke 1:45, in contrast to Zechariah's unbelief: "You will remain dumb, because you did not believe.")

She refers to the Son of God (Luke 1:32, 35), Lord (Luke 1:43; 2:11) and Savior (Luke 2:11, etc.). It is to God that Mary gives thanks in the *Magnificat* (but not without being identified, it seems, with his Son Jesus the Savior):

"My soul magnifies the Lord, and my spirit rejoices in God my Savior." This is a reference to the name of Jesus— *Yeshoua* means "God Saves," which here seems to refer to the Hebrew (Luke 1:46–47).

In the wake of the annunciation, she seems to identify her own son with God. She recognizes the richness of God's gift within her. Because of this free gift, "All generations will call me blessed," she prophesies. But she knows that this gift comes from God alone, because he has looked upon her lowliness: "He has looked with favor on the lowliness of his servant...for the Mighty One has done great things for me" (Luke 1:28–49).

Mary prophesies that this good news and grace, granted in her lowliness, will be extended to all the poor. Paradoxically, she says this in the *aorist* tense (a form of past tense in Greek), by prophetic anticipation, and by doing so shows her link to the Daughter of Zion along with the rest of the people, especially the poor:

> He has shown strength with his arm;
>   he has scattered the proud in the thoughts of
>   their hearts.
> He has brought down the powerful from their thrones,
>   and lifted up the lowly. (Luke 1:51–53)

The momentum of the visitation and the prophecy in the *Magnificat* show Mary's faith and overflow into gifts that manifest the efficient and operational power of God. These texts round out all that the Synoptic Gospels have to say: it is not the ties of flesh that somehow link us to God, but listening to and internalizing the Word of God and the gifts of the Spirit. The context seemed to imply that this grace had escaped Jesus' blood family, who had an intrusive approach. His own relatives are presented as "outsiders" in contrast to those inside the circle of the disciples (Mark 3:31–32).

In a similar context, John states that "not even his brothers believed in him" (John 7:5). This general statement is misleading. Luke tried to teach us, first, that Jesus' brothers had a prominent place in the primitive community after Pentecost (Acts 1:14), and second, that the first bishop of Jerusalem, James, was a "brother of the Lord" (Acts 12:17; 15:13; 21:18) and had great authority. Hegesippus (quoted by Eusebius in *Ecclesiastical History* 2:23, and confirmed by Flavius Josephus in *Antiquities of the Jews* 20:9:1) states that James was stoned to death in the cause of Christ. We also know the importance that Paul placed on him (Gal 2:9–11). Hegesippus (quoted by Eusebius in *Ecclesiastical History* 2:22:4) reports that Simeon, another "brother of the Lord," succeeded him as the second bishop of Jerusalem in AD 62. Hegesippus calls this brother "cousin": *anepsios.*

Luke tries to supply more detail about Mary (probably from the same family environment): her vocation (Luke 1:28–38), her faith (Luke 1:45), and her spiritual radiance (Luke 1:35, 39–56). From the beginning of his Gospel, he places Mary in the foreground as one who "hears the Word of God" consciously and reflectively, who "keeps it" (Luke 2:19) and radiates it (Luke 1:39–55). This is why he omits the superficial and ambiguous contrast in Mark 3:31–33, between Jesus' family and his disciples, as those "without" and those "within" the inner circle of the kingdom. It is within the family that listening to the Word and communion with Christ begins.

The story of the annunciation stipulates that the gift of grace is activated by the coming of the Spirit upon Mary (Luke 1:35). In my semiotic study, I have established the basic "scheme" that reflects the essential concept in Luke 1—2 (see Figure 1).

Figure 1

Law — Grace

No grace — No law

We must not forget that Grace = Spirit (Luke 1:28, 30; Luke 1:35; cf. 1:13, 41, 67).

Mary is therefore present in Christ and at the foundation of salvation, in terms not only of the flesh but of the Spirit, not only bodily—psychologically—but theologically. She is called to participate at the point of origin itself, as a founding member who is the first to welcome Christ, by hearing the Word and by dynamically receiving the Spirit. This is why the Church fathers very quickly recognized her as a type of the Church. Here lies the very foundation of her presence. It is the fundamental premise of Luke. But Luke's Gospel does not speak of Mary beyond the infancy narrative (Luke 2:51), except that the so-called anti-mariological flavor of the Synoptic Gospels appears to be softened by him. Nevertheless, he provides no positive addition apart from what is laid out in Luke 1—2.

In this regard, John forms a valuable complement to Luke, because he locates Mary positively in the public life and the passion of Christ. In a certain sense, he provides the missing puzzle piece needed to construct a theology of the Virgin Mary and of her presence.

JOHN 2:1–12

John affirms the active presence of Mary at the marriage feast at Cana and describes how she intervened (John 2:4); she remains confident and invites the servants to do everything that the Lord says (2:5). In this episode, her faith is engaged in a similar way to the visitation. And this first miracle that she asks of Jesus, in which she asks the servants to participate, is the very foundation of the disciples' faith.

> Jesus did this, the first of his signs, in Cana of Galilee, and revealed his glory; and his disciples believed in him. (2:11)

This scene is very important. According to what the Gospel itself says, it is a theophany, as announced in John 1:51 (the last verse of the previous chapter):

> Very truly, I tell you, you will see heaven opened and the angels of God ascending and descending upon the Son of Man.

It is a new covenant sealed by the first miracle and the faith of the disciples. This covenant is identified with the one on Sinai, and is celebrated by the Feast of Pentecost. The miracle at Cana is presented as a Pentecost. It is for this reason that John places it on the "third day" (John 2:1; Exod 19:11, 10, 16), which is expanded by numerous texts of the Jewish tradition studied by A. Serra.[7]

In this new covenant, Mary, the Daughter of Zion, plays the eschatological role of the people, whose consent is important:

> All the words that the LORD has spoken we will do. (Exod 24:3, 7)

> Do whatever he tells you. (John 2:5)

Mary echoes these words. Her faith, hope, and intercession bring the beginning of Jesus' ministry forward, as the sign and the faith of the new covenant. The Gospel of John sees this as a specific character of the female role. Each of the three books of his Gospel—the Book of Signs (2—10), the Book of the Passion (11—19), and the Book of the Resurrection (20—21)—opens with two episodes involving women, each of which acts to usher in what comes thereafter: First, the words of Mary at Cana and the words of the Samaritan woman, which awaken faith in his people (John 4:29–30, 39); second, Martha's intercession that Jesus resurrect Lazarus (the prototype of the resurrection of Jesus) (John 11:20–44) and Mary's prophetic anointing of Jesus at Bethany, prefiguring Christ's burial (John 11:55–57); and third, Mary Magdalene's visit to the empty tomb, which was rewarded with the first appearance of Jesus (John 20).

Mary's inaugural role is not a unique and singular privilege exclusive to her alone. Other women play a similar role in John 4:11–12, 20. And this corresponds to John's anthropology. This anthropology, which we can also perceive in Luke, is at the root of the Gospel, where there is no discrimination between men and women, but rather a certain feminine priority that itself is terribly misunderstood. This cuts short from the outset feminist slogans that maintain that the Church only exalts Mary in order to belittle all other women (the pure contrasted with the impure, the Virgin contrasted with Gomer the prostitute [Hos 1:3]). This finding likewise destroys the assertion that women are reduced to a passive role in Christianity; this is the exact opposite of what the Gospel says.

Mary's role is no longer presented in contrast with that of sinful women, which is a typical complaint, but in the same proactive role as that of the other women: it is a defining trait. We no longer need to say, with F. M. Braun,[8] that the words of Jesus at Cana begin a separation between Mary and Jesus that lasts until his "hour" on Calvary: "My hour has not yet come" (John 2:4).

According to Braun, Jesus temporarily breaks his link with Mary during the time of his public ministry and goes with the Twelve. This interpretation completely misses the last verse of the Cana passage (2:12) that speaks not of separation, but, rather, of the journey they will make together, in order to stay together at Capernaum. "After this he went down to Capernaum with his mother, his brothers, and his disciples; and they remained there a few days" (John 2:12). Here we notice a parallel with Acts 1:14—in the context of Pentecost, John gives first place to the family, Jesus' mother and brothers, over the disciples.

It is surprising that Braun does not mention John 2:12. How can his 216-page book—devoted solely to the *Mother of the faithful* in the Gospel of John, which has only nine verses that mention Mary (1:13; 2:1, 3, 4, 5, 12; 19:25–27)—only mention eight verses and omit and contradict the ninth, which doesn't even appear in his list? This shows how an ideology, excellent as Braun's theology was, can cause blindness and a turning away from the objectivity necessary for exegesis.

Braun's interpretation is based on a sound and interesting observation: Jesus does not call Mary "mother," but "woman" (John 2:4; 12:26), just like the Samaritan woman (John 4:21), the Canaanite woman (Matt 15:28), the woman caught in adultery (John 28:10), the crippled woman (Luke 13:12), or Mary Magdalene (John 20:13). Braun paraphrases:

> My ability to work this miracle does not come from you. But that through which I must suffer I have received from you. This is why I will know you when my weakness is suspended on the Cross....My hour has not yet come: but when the hour of my Passion comes, I will know you as my Mother, and so it is that, hanging on the Cross, he entrusted his mother to his disciple.[9]

This is a good commentary, and is suggestive, but again it is inaccurate, because when Jesus is on the Cross he does not renew his ties to his mother, but rather, as we shall see, he transfers them. He will make Mary the mother of the disciple at the time of his death and she will lose him.

JOHN 2 AND 19: AN INCLUSION

It is important to stress the strict correlation between Cana (John 2:1–12) and the episode at Calvary (John 19:25–27). These two episodes correspond to each other according to the Semitic method of inclusion in which a recurring theme at the beginning and at the end expresses the sense of the whole.

The inclusion of most of John's Gospel between Cana (the opening scene involving a woman) and Calvary (the closing scene involving a woman) becomes noticeable in many ways. In both sections, Mary is referred to as "the mother of Jesus" (anonymously). But Jesus calls her "woman" (John 2:4; 19:26). Likewise, in both sections, Jesus' hour (the decisive moment that is both the hour of his death and the hour of his glory) is mentioned—John 2:4: "My 'hour' has not yet come" and John 19:27: "from that 'hour' the disciple took her into his own home." The first verse corresponds to the second. Braun clearly sees that Jesus refers back to Mary at the appointed "hour" par excellence. Cana and Calvary also correspond to each other as inauguration and consummation. John 2:11: "Jesus did this, the first of his signs, in Cana of Galilee" and John 19:28: "After this, when Jesus knew that all was now finished, [*tete lestai*] he said (in order to fulfill [*teleiôthé*] the scripture), 'I am thirsty'...he said, 'It is finished [*Tetelestai*].'"

The fact that these passages involve a woman is important. Masculinity and femininity cannot be dissociated from one another or ignored. They are interrelated and involved in one another in reality, just as they are in the Gospel. But the Gospel has highlighted the specific importance and the positive nature of the female role. The Gospel clearly recognizes the female role of initiation and anticipation. Elizabeth was the first to recognize God's grace, before her husband, Zechariah, who remained mute because he refused to believe (Luke 1:39–45). In the Gospel of John, the Samaritan woman ushers in the proclamation of the gospel as we see in 4:39–42; Martha and Mary anticipate the mystery of the resurrection (11:21–57; 12:1–8). Mary Magdalene goes before the apostles to the empty tomb and is the first to see the resurrected Christ. Mary is the first of this line of inaugurations and anticipations, at the annunciation and the visitation (Luke 1:28–56), just as at Cana (2:1–12). She is marked by the pure impulse that makes her the first to desire and receive the gift of God. Mary, who has been associated with Christ in her role as a woman, continues to witness to it in the Church. She has developed the potentialities inherent in her position as a woman and mother: not just as a mother, but as a woman whose attributes are not limited to her motherly role. The inauguration is the bringing together or completion that John emphatically denotes by using two teleological words: *teleô*, in 19:28 and 30, for the fulfillment of the hour; and *teleiô*, in 19:28, for the fulfillment of Scriptures.

Additionally, these two scenes at Cana and Cavalry are theophanies, or divine manifestations of Christ. In the first one, Jesus "revealed his glory" (John 2:11) through an anticipatory sign. In the second, he manifests the completion in line with John's fundamental theological theme: his glory is his being lifted up on the cross (3:23; 8:28; 12:32–34) and his death itself (cf. John 11:40; 17:5, 24). The multiple uses of the verb *to glorify* refer to his tragic end (7:39; 11:4; 12:16, 23, 28; 13:31–32; 14:13; 17:1, 4–5, 10).

Finally, both scenes end with the theme of Mary dwelling with the disciples. John 2:12: "After this he went down to Capernaum with his mother, his brothers, and his disciples; and they remained there [*emeinan*] a few days," and 19:27: "And from that hour the disciple took her into his own home." But when we compare the opening and closing scenes, we find that Mary's role is different in each. At Cana she plays an active anticipatory role, just as in John's other five scenes regarding women, while at Calvary she passively receives a new maternal role and becomes detached from Christ, at the hour of his death, by her maternity being transferred. This transfer is vividly expressed by the play of the Greek possessive pronouns, which unfortunately is lost in translation (highlighted in italics below):

> Meanwhile, standing near the cross of Jesus were *his* mother [and the two other Marys]. When Jesus saw *the* mother and the disciple whom he loved standing beside her, he said to *the* mother, "Woman, here is your son." Then he said to the disciple, "Here is *your* mother." And from that hour the disciple took her into his own home. (John 19:25–27)

Unlike in the other Gospels, Mary alone is present at Calvary, at the decisive hour of completion. This, then, is how Jesus gives birth to the new people in the person of the "disciple whom he loved," and to the Church, symbolized by the water and the blood (John 19:34), coming from his open side, in which the Church fathers have seen the sacraments of the new covenant. In this birth, Mary has a figurative and symbolic role. What role is that? Should we call her Mother of the Church? That would be to say more than the Evangelist, because for him it is Christ who gives birth to the Church, coming out of the temple of his body, from which flows the fountain of living water, at the same time as he also "delivers" the spirit of life through his death. Mary participates in this mystery as mother of the disciples, but she does not play the key role.

John assigns Mary a multiple role, in the same sense as Luke. For him it is a triple role. First, as the mother of Jesus. This leitmotiv remains fundamental (2:1, 3, 5, 12; 19:25–27). Second, as the Daughter of Zion. As we have seen, she is presented as such in the episode at Cana, where she repeats the words of God's people, which seal the first covenant: "Do whatever he tells you" (2:5). At Calvary, she assumes the same role as Daughter of Zion, mother to the new people in accordance with Micah 4:9–10 and, above all, Isaiah 66:7–11.

> Before she was in labor
>   she gave birth;
> before her pain came upon her
>   she delivered a son.
> Who has heard of such a thing?
>   Who has seen such things?
> Shall a land be born in one day?
>   Shall a nation be delivered in one moment?
> Yet as soon as Zion was in labor
>   she delivered her children.
> Shall I open the womb and not deliver?
>   says the LORD;
> shall I, the one who delivers, shut the womb?
>   says your God.
>
> Rejoice with Jerusalem, and be glad for her,
>   all you who love her;
> rejoice with her in joy,
>   all you who mourn over her—
> that you may nurse and be satisfied
>   from her consoling breast;
> that you may drink deeply with delight
>   from her glorious bosom. (Isa 66:7–11)

John 16:21 (which has been studied in depth by A. Feuillet) also uses this text in reference to John 19:25–27:

> When a woman is in labor, she has pain, because her hour has come. But when her child is born, she no longer remembers the anguish because of the joy of having brought a human being into the world. So you have pain now; but I will see you again, and your hearts will rejoice, and no one will take your joy from you.

The theme of Isaiah 66 is repeated at Qumran and in Revelation 12, which confirms the convergence of the Johannine tradition.

In her third role as the new Eve, Mary is called, paradoxically, "woman" (and not mother). Jesus is referring to the woman in Genesis 3. As Hoskyns perceived many years ago, John refers the saving passion of Christ to the fall in Genesis 3. It is because of this symbolism that he locates Jesus' arrest (John 18:1), and his entombment, in a garden:

> Now there was a garden in the place where he was crucified, and in the garden there was a new tomb in which no one had ever been laid. (John 19:41)

Here we have, once again, an inclusion.

Among these allusions, which we have no room to go into here, there is less reference to Mary as the enemy of the serpent (Gen 3:15) or as giving birth in pain (Gen 3:16), although these references, which are obvious in Revelation 12, may still be an undercurrent here. She is especially compared to Eve as "mother of the living" (Gen 3:20), through her new adoptive motherhood (cf. Rev 12:17). This theme is located in reference to the life that was the purpose of Jesus' ministry: "That they may have life and have it abundantly" (John 10:10).

JOHN 19:25–27

If we evaluate the convergences between John 2 and 19, we find a commentary that is sufficient for our purposes. The main conclusions are Mary's presence as mother, from Cana to Calvary, and the fact that her presence with Christ is consistent with her presence with humankind: the guests at the marriage feast at Cana for whom she intercedes (John 2:3), the servants whom she directs toward Jesus (2:5), his brothers and disciples she lived with (John 2:12), and the disciple whom she adopts as a type for all the disciples and with whom she came to live (John 19:27). All this indicates a close link between Mary's presence with Christ (which was not without trials: the separation of his public life, the detachment and suffering of Calvary) and her presence with humankind, or, more formally, with the disciples.

The precedence of the formula, "Woman behold your son" (John 19:26) over the formula, "Son behold your mother" (John 19:27) indicates that it is not a matter of the disciples' filial piety welcoming Mary, who has been abandoned, so much as an adoption entrusted to her as an extension of her role at Cana, at the beginning of the ministry, as a foundation of the disciples' faith, looking toward the "hour" of Jesus. Briefly, Mary's bond with Jesus is inseparable from her bond with the people of God, as Daughter of Zion, and probably as a counterpart to Eve (Luke and John).

LUKE AND JOHN

Luke and John seem to complement each other perfectly: Luke locates Mary in the infancy narrative and does not mention her again even in the genealogy that began Jesus' public life, in chapter 3 (unlike Matthew, he is less interested in the roles of women and of Mary), and John locates her within Christ's ministry, both at its inauguration and at its conclusion on Calvary. Luke has Mary as part of Jesus' hidden life, John as part of his public life; in Luke Mary's role is at his birth, while in John it is at his death. But the contrast is not so clear-cut. Both Gospels converge more than it seems, and overlap each other on the missing part of each, which tends to confirm that they are rooted in a common tradition.

John does not forget Christ's origins; the incarnation. He begins here in his Prologue, and develops this theme by constant reference to Luke 1—2.[10] Resch pointed out these numerous points of contact in 1897 and I have gone back over them twice. Briefly, Luke's and John's Prologues have the same structure: in both cases, it is a parallel that makes the contrast between John the Baptist and Jesus the Messiah, Son of God. Jesus alone is the light (Luke 1:78; 2:32; John 1:7–9) and John the Baptist is only a witness to that light (Luke 1:76–78; John 1—7). In both texts, Jesus is identified as the Glory of God (Luke 2:32; John 1:14). He came "to his own" and "his own did not receive him" (Luke 2:7; John 1:10). If we use this framework, we can see that the formula contained in John 1:13 on the origin of the "Word made flesh" is presented as an echo of Luke 1:34.

Luke 1:34–35	John 1:13–14
"How can this be, since I am a virgin?"	Born, not of blood or of the will of the flesh
The power of the Most High	or of the will of man, but of God.
will overshadow you;	And the Word lived among us [literally
he will be called Son of God.	"pitched his tent among us"],
The child grew and became strong, filled with wisdom; and the favor of God was upon him.	father's only son, full of grace and truth.

The points of contact here go beyond the actual phrases used: Jesus is God alone, in both texts, his bodily presence is indicated by the expressions that are usually employed when describing the ark of the covenant. It is the image of the *Shekinah*, referring to the tabernacle; the place covered by God's shadow and filled with his presence as 1:35 states, referring back to Exodus 40:35; God's dwelling place where God pitches his tent (his tabernacle [*eskenosên*]) among his people, as per John 1:13.

Should John 1:13 be read as singular—"He who is

born"—or plural—"those who have been born"? According
to the commentary of J. Galot, P. Hofritchter, and I. de la
Potterie, the Church fathers from the first centuries tend to
read it as singular. It is the same for the point of contact
between John 1 and Luke 1. But whatever the solution to
the problem may be, as we have already discussed, John's
Prologue marks the progression from the eternal birth of the
Word, the Son of God (John 1:14, 18) to his temporal
birth—which can be clearly seen from John 1:13—and baptismal birth through faith (John 1:12 and maybe also 13).
The important thing is to understand the Johannine perspective. He is not speaking of three births, as we have it
nowadays, but, if we go by his perspective, of one birth that
progresses in time, as the fathers of the Church well knew:
his birth is eternal in origin and becomes temporal at
Christmas and baptismal for Christians. This is undoubtedly
the reason why it was ambiguous whether to read these first
texts as singular or plural. It only affects the way in which
we refer to the temporal birth of Christ and the theological
birth of the Christian, respectively. In any case, the birth of
the Word is referred to in all its aspects. And John responds
synthetically, in laying out his initial theological thoughts, by
echoing the infancy narrative contained in Luke 1—2 (not
that of Matt 1—2).

As for Luke, he does not ignore Jesus' public life and
the separation that it causes between Jesus and Mary, in
Luke 8:19–20 and 11:27–28, just as in John 2:4. He also
refers to Mary's suffering at the passion: Simeon's prophecy,
"a sword will pierce your own soul too" (Luke 2:35), signifies the climax of contradictions experienced by Christ in
his passion. And this pain, predicted for Mary, finds its full
realization that is highly symbolic of the passion. In the
episode of finding the child Jesus in the temple, Mary
loses Jesus and searches for him for three days in
Jerusalem, during the Feast of the Passover, in the same
city in which he will disappear for three days in the tomb,

during another Passover feast. The word used by Mary to describe the pains of those three days is "anxiety": "Your father and I have been searching for you in great *anxiety*" (Luke 2:48). The word *odynomenoi* used here is the same word used to describe the torture of hellfire for the rich man in Luke 16:24–25, the experience of Paul's disciples on hearing of his death (Acts 20:38), and the mortal suffering of Paul for the Jewish people—so unbearable that he would wish to be cut off and damned himself if he could save his people (Rom 9:2). The convergences are well captured by the fathers of the Church and refer to the death of Christ. All this would become clear in the most coherent way if Luke (or his source) knew the Johannine tradition about Mary's being present at Calvary, and if he referred to this event in the prophecy about her suffering, the effects of which Mary will experience both symbolically and actually when she seeks out her son who has already been lost at the Passover when he is twelve years old.[11]

There are other convergences: Mary's detachment from Jesus between John 2:13 and 19:25, which has its parallel in Luke; and also the infancy narrative. While Mary played an active and central role in the annunciation-visitation (Luke 1:26–58, where she is the focus, the heroine, when analyzed semiotically), she finds a modest, silent, negligible role in chapter 2, apart from the brief episode where she brings Jesus into the world, wraps him in swaddling clothes, and lays him in the manger. Before and after that, all the active roles in chapter 2 belong to other characters.

It is the shepherds who arrive in haste (Luke 2:16) and no longer Mary, as at the visitation. It is they who spread the good news, that is to say the gospel (Luke 2:17–18). In 2:21 where Luke, with great solemnity, tells us how Jesus receives his name, "The name given by the angel before he was conceived in the womb," he completely obscures Mary, whose role it was to give him his name. This name disappears completely between 2:20 and 33. In the episode of the Presentation in the Temple, she receives the painful prophecy about the sword passively. And it is the prophetess Anna who, like the shepherds, plays an active role in announcing the good news (Luke 2:38). Jesus is handed over to Simeon who announces the trial that lies ahead (Luke 2:28). And Mary will have a first taste of that trial when Jesus leaves her to stay at the temple. Mary does not understand (Luke 2:50), but welcomes the trial in faith and ponders it in her heart (Luke 2:51; cf. 2:19). Everything happens as if the child had been given to her only to be snatched away again. She does not act as a possessive mother, she does not worry; for a whole day, she thinks of his disappearance as normal in such a huge caravan of travelers (Luke 2:44–46).

These historical overlaps and the three theological convergences—(1) the role of the virginal conception in the incarnation, (2) the reference to Mary at the passion, and (3) the distance between her and her Son, which she accepts—give solidity to the structural reconstitution that will follow, together with their convergence with Mary Mother of Christ, Daughter of Zion.

ACTS 1:14

There is more: Luke is silent on the subject of Mary in the public life and passion of Jesus, in keeping with his way of finishing up with a character, and he stops foreshadowing future events. Luke goes further than John. He prolongs the narrative. In John 19:27, after the episode of Calvary, Mary disappears. In Luke (who seems to have forgotten about her after the infancy narrative, apart from a few insignificant references in Luke 8, 11), she reappears at Pentecost in 1:14.

And she has the same kind of presence there that she had in Luke 1. Reference is made to the Holy Spirit coming upon her, as in Luke 1:35. In Acts 1:8, there is an outpouring that fills the Church and Mary herself (Acts 2:4), just as it filled John the Baptist (Luke 1:15) and Elizabeth (Luke 1:41; cf. Zech 1:67) when Mary visited her. Vatican II highlighted this pneumatological closeness. In Luke, there is a sort of inclusion, from the birth of Christ to the birth of the Church, which in a certain way mirrors the Johannine inclusion between the first miracle (Cana, Luke 2:12) and the fulfillment (John 19:25–30, which is of similar pneumatological importance). But in Luke, the inclusion is wider—Mary encompasses the history of salvation, from the birth of Christ (Luke 1—2) to the birth of the Church (Acts 1—2).

Finally, Mary has a role as a sign, in both Luke and John, as well as explicitly in Isaiah 7:14 and Acts 12:1. We will return to this later.

GENESIS AND THE STRUCTURE OF MARY'S PRESENCE IN THE NEW TESTAMENT

Mary is present through the story of salvation in various episodes and traces that we must now summarize.

BEFORE CHRIST—THE FIRST TIME OF SEPARATION

Mary, the Daughter of Zion, is first presented as the fulfillment of Israel (Daughter of Zion) through grace (Luke 1:28, 30) and faith (Luke 1:45), and through the gift that is given to her of the Messiah, Son of God. In accepting this gift through her theological faith (Luke 1:45), she sums up and fulfills the whole ascent of Israel. She fulfills expectation.

All this is accomplished in the knowledge of the Scriptures that weave into the story the message received by Mary, and the *Magnificat*, in which she expresses her thanks (Luke 1:46–56). The good news of the annunciation fulfills all of Scripture: the birth of the Messiah and the eschatological coming of the Lord himself. It is the Son of God who transcendently fulfills the role promised to the messianic heir of David. This coming together of pure grace, through which God goes beyond what was expected, places Mary in a prominent position, which is without parallel anywhere else in Scripture. We can see the role that is given to her at both the annunciation and the visitation in Luke 1:35, 42–45, 46–49.[12]

Mary, therefore, anticipates the coming of Christ throughout all of her youth, right up to the annunciation (which, according to an unsubstantiated pious tradition, occurred when she was fifteen years old). Everything is accomplished through grace (Luke 1:28, 30), but Mary's active reflection (Luke 1:29, 34) and determination (Luke 1:39, 44–56) are remarkable.

THE HIDDEN LIFE AND THE FIRST EXPERIENCE OF COMMUNION

At the annunciation, Mary accepts the coming of Christ and of God himself, because the Son is announced to her as both divine and human. Her free consent through faith, the complete availability of her body and spirit, form an integral part of this mystery. They are inseparable. Her unique role represents both the ancient people (as Daughter of Zion) and the new (as a type of the Church).

She does not share this physical task with Joseph—"I am a virgin" (Luke 1:34)—despite the link between her intrinsic motherly role and the role of adoptive father assigned to Joseph (Luke 2; Matt 1:18–25). Her role as mother constitutes a charism, in the strongest sense of the word. According to Saint Paul and classical theology, the charisms are defined as free gifts given for the edification of the Church. Here then we are dealing with the first charism, given for the edification of the body of Christ: the physical body, the origin and principle of the mystical body.

The fact that Mary forms the physical body of Christ (the human foundation of the incarnation) is obvious. The fact that she founds the mystical body is also clear, because she gives Christ the first profession of theological faith (Luke 1:45). If the Son of God becomes man by dwelling within Mary's body, Mary is the first member of Christ's body through her communion of faith (Luke 1:38). Through her, Christ is introduced into the human race, into the people of God, into humanity, in order to save it from within. He receives from her this human condition in which he becomes priest and victim. Mary does not only form his body. She also plays the same role as any mother in the formation of his mind. This begins in the life-giving bond of gestation, where the human being can already hear the beat of his mother's heart, as psychological tests have shown. After birth, the mother is the first human face through which the child learns to know others, which Virgil tellingly expresses in his Fourth Eclogue:

Incipe, parve puer risu cognoscere matrem. (Learn, little boy, to recognize your mother with a smile.)

Virgil does not stipulate whether the infant learns to know the mother by seeing her smile or whether it is by smiling at the mother (by reflecting her smile) that he learns to know her. In fact, there is no need to separate the two. The awareness is bilateral, reciprocal. Mary plays the same physical and psychological role that all mothers play. And this role is no less present in the humanity of the Son of God.

So it is this first phase of communion that lasts a long time, from the annunciation (conception and the beginning of gestation) right up to Jesus' public life. It is the hidden life of Jesus, a poor life (Luke 2:24), in which Jesus' parents make an offering that the poor would make at the temple. It encompasses sharing a stable at Bethlehem (Luke 2:7), the exile in Egypt, according to Matthew 2:13–20, then the hardscrabble life of the underdeveloped times in which Jesus lived. We can guess at the internal variety of this long period: gestation, a sudden journey, the discomfort of Bethlehem, the flight into Egypt, the return to Nazareth, and a hardworking life until he was thirty (Luke 2:23).

During this long phase of communion, a first episode of separation occurs when Jesus is lost and eventually found in the temple. Luke says that this separation lasted three days, which, of course, prefigures the death of Christ. According to him, Mary, in contemplating these events, and her three days of anxiety in search of Jesus, receives the first taste of the sword that Simeon mentioned, and we have the first indication of the passion, where the two infancy narratives (Matthew and Luke) cast their shadow across Jesus' hidden life.

JESUS' PUBLIC LIFE—THE SECOND TIME OF SEPARATION

Jesus' ministry constitutes a long separation after thirty years of family life: Jesus fasts in the desert and then leads an itinerant life with his disciples. A group of women formed part of his disciples (Luke 8:1–3), but Mary was not among them. She remains involved in the family. Mark symbolically contrasts Jesus' "mother and brothers" who are "outside" (Mark 3:31–32; cf. Matt 12:46–47; Luke 8:20) with the circle of disciples surrounding him (Mark 3:34; cf. 3:32; those who were sitting around him). Jesus looks "at those who sat around him" (Mark 3:34). His word is for those in the inner circle rather than those outside. This is a contrast that remains blurred in Luke.

But the separation is not complete. Mary meets Jesus, at the start of his ministry, at the marriage feast at Cana. This seems to suggest to her the trial of separation that his public ministry will involve. He is not taking time off from his ministry, as F. M. Braun would have it. After this first sign, he remains for a few days at Capernaum "with his mother, his brothers and his disciples." His mother and brothers are mentioned first. His mother will see him again when he returns to Nazareth (Matt 4:13; Luke 4:16). She is present with his family when they come to seize him— they were probably motivated by an issue to do with clan obligations (Mark 3:20, 31–35).

COMMUNION AT THE CRUCIFIXION—THE SECOND EXPERIENCE OF COMMUNION

Mary comes to Jesus again at Golgotha, after the separation of his public life. She comes to him no longer during his hidden life, but through his public condemnation and the suffering of being exposed to public ridicule; no longer in the humility of the poor, but in the humiliation of the condemned, which is torturous for all of his family who have been affected by such misfortune. It is "the hour" of fulfillment (John 19:28–30). Mary, who is linked to the initial kenosis of the Son of God made man, comes back to him now through an even more mysterious and dramatic kenosis: that of the just man crucified. Her presence, standing at the foot of the cross (John 19:25), shows the persistence of her faith, which was irreversibly engaged at the annunciation (Luke 1:38, 45). The perfection of her holiness (Luke 1:28, 35, 45) and her communion with Christ are signs of her participation in the mystery of redemption.

Without doubt the *redemption itself* is the work of Christ alone, since he alone is God; he alone is condemned, wounded, martyred. He alone dies, is resurrected, returns to the Father, and sends the Spirit. But he wanted the presence of Mary, who is lovingly united to this "work" as at the incarnation. She is united to the cross, through her communion as mother, touched by the sufferings of her Son and through his theological communion with her. And nothing prevents her flawless holiness from being joined to the founding work of redemption. As a human being, as a woman, as a redeemed person, as she stands by Christ's side, she represents all the human values that he has not personally taken upon himself. Her participation was not necessary, but she responds freely to God's plan to involve humanity in every stage and aspect of salvation. Here we are speaking of the most profound role that Mary plays in her participation in the history of salvation, on humanity's behalf. The new mission that Christ's mother receives is marked by the sign of death. For her it is the hour of being transfixed by compassion; the sufferings of her Son touch Mary's heart (Luke 2:35). And instead of consolation, Jesus gives her the pains of motherhood so eloquently expressed by the play of possessive pronouns that we have already pointed out: the mother of Jesus, "his mother," becomes an empty motherhood through grief, "the mother"; and through the will of Jesus, "the mother of the Disciple" and of all his disciples: "Here is your mother."

FROM DEATH TO THE ASSUMPTION: THE GREAT SEPARATION

Christ's death gives rise to a new separation, of the most heartbreaking kind. The details of this separation are complex, diverse, productive, and full of meaning.

The Triduum Mortis

According to the ancient medieval tradition, during the triduum mortis, Mary's faith ensures that there is continuity on earth between the sinful world, which has put

Christ to death, and his resurrection. This is what is symbolized by the last paschal candle still burning in the darkness. It is not extinguished, but instead is hidden for awhile
behind the altar before being replaced on the candlestick.
It is Mary's faith, which is the only light still burning in the
night that has fallen on Golgotha (Matt 27:45 and parallel
texts). Mary's prayer is an extension of Christ's and is the
seed of the prayer of the Pentecost community, where she
was like a living flame.[13]

The Forty Days of Apparitions

We will not attempt to explain the Gospels' silence on
Mary's presence during the time in which Christ appeared
to the disciples (nor speculate on whether she was present
at the Last Supper). It seems likely that Mary was present
when the apparitions took place. According to John she
was in Jerusalem when the passion took place (John
19:25–27), and according to Luke it seems that she did not
leave town until the time of the ascension and Pentecost
(Acts 1:14). She was, therefore, present for some of Christ's
apparitions—at least the one witnessed by five hundred of
the brethren, which Paul speaks about in 1 Corinthians
15:6 (could this refer to the ascension, before they entered
the upper room?) (Acts 1:8–14). It is a fact, however, that
the Gospel is silent on the matter and only attributes
apparitions to the women disciples—principally Mary
Magdalene, but not Mary (the apparition to Mary Magdalene,
a woman, is mentioned by only two of the evangelists:
Matt 29:9–10; John 20:11, 18). Their silence could pertain
to the fact that the evangelists essentially value only the
apparitions to the Twelve, who are Christ's official witnesses; only male witnesses had full value legally. We will
respect the discretion of the evangelists and will not raise
any controversy (which often arises) on the first apparition, which John Chrysostom, Ephraim, and various other

fathers attribute to Mary and assume that there is some confusion with Mary Magdalene.[14]

Waiting for Pentecost (Acts 1:14)

Over and above the forty days silence during which the risen Christ appeared to his disciples, we find it again in the upper room with the first Christian community:

> All these were constantly devoting themselves [*omothymadon*] to prayer, together with certain women [the female disciples spoken about in Luke 8:1–3], including Mary the mother of Jesus [*têi mêtri Iésou*], as well as his brothers.

Only Mary is named along with the eleven disciples. She is located at the intersection of the two groups of disciples—women and family—because she belongs to both. She is with them in prayer. She awaits Christ's promise, the Holy Spirit (Acts 1:8), who will change this praying community into the Church.

Mary finds a role that is symmetrical with that of the annunciation going into this new transition: she is no longer before Christ, but after the life of Christ, and on the threshold of the time of the Holy Spirit, who will identify that community with Christ.

Pentecost

At Pentecost, Mary is baptized in the Holy Spirit along with the hundred and twenty disciples of the primitive Church (Acts 1:14; 2:1–13). Mary is involved in the community of the upper room: "*All* of them were filled with the Holy Spirit and began to speak in other languages…"

Mary is included in that *all*, but can she receive the Holy Spirit? She had already received it at the annunciation, when the Holy Spirit came upon her (Luke 1:35); she was the first to receive it, in order to welcome the Son of God made man. It would seem that she did not receive it this time. However this objection is groundless, since, according to Acts itself, the apostles were "filled with the Holy Spirit" on the day of Pentecost (Acts 2:4; cf. 1:5; 11:16) and are "filled" again in Acts 4:31: "The place in which they were gathered together was shaken; and they were all filled with the Holy Spirit."

They were already filled. How could they be filled again? The reason is that they were about to take the next step, to experience a new trial: persecution. It is the same for Mary: the outpouring of the Spirit can be renewed again and again (in contrast to the rite of baptism that can only be received once, since its underlying purpose is to unite the Christian to the Church).

Did Mary receive a new outpouring of the charisms? She exercised the charism of prophecy at the visitation, and others, beginning with her charism of mother of the Lord. If we take Acts 2 literally, she was included in the gift of glossolalia, which was a prominent sign of the new outpouring: "All of them were filled with the Holy Spirit and began to speak in other languages, as the Spirit gave them ability" (Acts 2:4). Mary is involved in the speaking in tongues that so amazed the crowd at Pentecost, before Peter explains in a language that everybody could understand (Acts 2:14).

Mary in the Primitive Church

At the annunciation, Mary alone was the seed and principle of the Church and began the communion of redeemed humanity in Christ. She already realized the essence of theological life and adherence to the Savior. She now becomes a member of the nascent Church, the visible Church; she is an unparalleled member, a founder member; she is humble but prefigures the Church's future. Cardinal Journet writes:

> She raised the nascent Church by the power of contemplation and love. This was more useful to the Church than the apostles who were acting outside of it. For the Church, she was the hidden root that draws up sap which bursts forth into flowers and fruit.[15]

This text essentially means that Mary's role in the Church is not to be through ministries and authority. Rather, she brings about the perfection of the Church through her divine and holy life.

How long was Mary present in the primitive Church? One pious tradition says fifteen years. This is nothing but a symbolic evaluation based on the following assumptions: Jesus lived for thirty-three years. Mary would have become his mother at the age of fifteen—the earliest she could have married—and she would have survived him by a symmetrical length of time of fifteen years, so she would have been sixty-three. This tradition has its origins in a letter of Evodius of Antioch and in the *Chronicon paschale*. On the basis of this, in 1884, a request had been put forward to the Congregation of Rites to celebrate the nineteenth centenary of the birth of the Virgin Mary. The Congregation of Rites replied, in *Acta Sanctae Sedis* 20 (1884): 525–27, that it could not consent because of a "lack of historical certainty on the dates." This seems to have discouraged petitions from those who wished to celebrate the second millennium of Mary's birth in 1982 (according to a slightly different computation).

WHERE DID SHE LIVE?

According to tradition, she lived in Jerusalem (based on Acts 1:14 and the archaeological discovery of the Virgin's tomb by Father Bagatti), but this seems to be superseded nowadays by the tradition of Ephesus, which suggests that Mary had followed John between 44 and 50.[16]

The Assumption and the Glorious Communion

The question remains: Do we need to look outside of the biblical field in order to pursue this further? We have already mentioned the Book of Revelation. But does it speak of Mary? Does it speak of the assumption? According to ancient tradition—which was reluctant to say that Mary suffered the pains of childbirth—and to modern secular exegesis, chapter 12 of Revelation speaks only of the Church. However, Revelation 12:5 gives us some evidence that it is about the mother of the Messiah:

> And she gave birth to a son, a male child, who is
> to rule all the nations with a rod of iron.

It is, therefore, certainly the personal mother of the Messiah who is referred to in such an obvious way. It makes no difference that she is also identified with the Church, since Luke and John (who is so strongly linked to Rev 12, of which he may be the author) identify Mary as the Daughter of Zion, the mother of both the Messiah and the new people mentioned in the Old Testament.

We should not be surprised that the pains of childbirth are mentioned in the symbolic context of Revelation. Christ appears in this context as the Lamb who is both glorious and sacrificed (or slaughtered: Rev 5:6–12; 13:8). So the mother of the Messiah can also appear both glorified and in pain: in heaven (11:19; 12:1) and in the pains of childbirth (12:2), which together signify the persecution of the Church (cf. 12:17).

What About the Assumption?

Father A. A. Jugie believes that the assumption is referred to in the "wings of a great eagle" that the woman receives "so that she could fly from the serpent into the wilderness to her place where she is nourished" (Rev 12:14).

But this suggestive symbolic conflation lacks exegetical consistency. F. M. Braun has based his more consistent hypothesis on Revelation 12:6:

> Her child was caught up to God and to his throne, while the woman fled into the wilderness, where God prepared a place for her to be fed for 1260 days (the 1260 = three-and-a-half years, the typical duration, borrowed from the book of Daniel 5:25 and 12:7. Here we find it again in Rev 11:2: forty-two months and in 12:14 where the woman likewise nourished "for a time, and times, and half a time," which is another way of expressing the same symbolic duration: 1+2+1/2).

The "place that is prepared" is, according to the Gospel of John, another name for heaven: "Where I am going, you cannot come," Jesus says in John 13:33. "In my Father's house there are many dwelling places. If it were not so, would I have told you that I go to prepare a place for you? And if I go and prepare a place for you, I will come again and will take you to myself, so that where I am, there you may be also" (14:2–3).

It is possible that this reference is true, but it is difficult to prove. What is clear is that Revelation 12 refers to both the joyful mystery of the incarnation and the sorrowful mystery of the death of Christ, which is identified with the persecution of Christians. The controversial issue of the attempt to kill the Messiah is (semiotically) identical to the theme in Matthew 2, Herod's attempt to kill the Messiah.

In Revelation, the glory that surrounds the woman, like the glory surrounding the Lamb, is representative of the birth of Christ and the passion, which form an integral part of the glory of Christ the Savior. The glory of Mary seems, then, in a certain sense, when taken symbolically, difficult to evaluate. It reflects the assumption, as does the liturgy (although, Pius XII refused to base its definition on this text). It teaches us nothing further on the matter and does not provide proof.

In Christian tradition, Revelation 12 illustrates Mary's presence in the Christian people. It is as the woman "clothed with the sun, with the moon under her feet" that she appeared at Guadalupe (December 12, 1531), the great shrine in Mexico whose role in founding the Church of Latin America is now recognized. Mary appeared to a Native American, in a Native American place, not to a bishop. And it was the Native American who commanded the bishop to build a shrine. Because of this it was an aboriginal Church that was founded, not a colonial one: the new people in the new world we recognize today.

Similarly, it is the woman from Revelation who is evoked in different ways, by the apparition at the Rue de Bac (1830) and (in a less obvious manner) at Lourdes (1858), where the Immaculate appeared clothed with the sun, according to the words of Saint Bernadette. The apparition was "shining like the sun," she stated.

"But no one can look at the sun!" we might object.

She explained: "No, like the sun when it is on the earth: I mean when its rays light up and transfigure objects."

In terms of Catholic faith, what is clear and is guaranteed in Pius XII's dogmatic definition is that Mary, "at the end of her earthly destiny," experienced communion with Christ, beyond the last trial of separation (the fourth after the finding in the temple, Jesus' public life, and the days following his death). It is unmitigated communion. Beyond the dark night of the soul, Mary receives from God full awareness and knowledge of her adopted children.

Beyond what can be gleaned explicitly from Scripture, but still in keeping with the dynamic indications encompassed from the annunciation to the marriage feast at Cana and in Revelation, Mary finds, with Christ and in him, the double role that John shows us at Cana: On the one hand, she anticipates Christ's desires and intercedes for humankind ("They have no wine" [John 2:3]); and on the other hand, she encourages us to service ("Do whatever he tells you" [John 2:5]).

She asks for the wine of the Holy Spirit for them and requires their attentive cooperation—this is a very good description of Mary's typical role in our lives. John the Evangelist seems to have taken on the symbolic meaning of these events that prefigure the role of Mary in the glory of Christ.

We are well placed to say, then, that Mary is present throughout the story of salvation: before, during, and after the life of Christ, according to the relevant time and context. She goes ahead of the Church in showing the fundamental faith of the New Testament in glory. She is united to Christ through an irreversible theological consent to God's will that spans times of trial and separation. No other human being is so thoroughly, profoundly, and universally integrated with the time of Salvation in so many different ways. No one else has been so deeply united to Christ the Savior and to humanity, so completely dedicated to the service of Christ the Savior and to the salvation of humankind. Through grace, she is committed to her role as saint, woman, and mother. Such is the presence of Mary in Scripture and in the history of salvation.

II
MARY'S PRESENCE IN THE LITURGY AND WORSHIP OF THE CHURCH

Mary's presence in Scripture is extended in a living and vibrant way within the life of the Church. Acts 1:14 tells us that, between the ascension and Pentecost, she occupied a specific place within the community that was not hierarchical in nature, but was nonetheless remarkable. During the time that the historical-critical method was popular, and close attention was paid to legalism and dogmas, I believed along with everyone else that Mary's presence in the Church was negligible up to the fourth century. However, this did not take into account the living tradition that then blossomed around the first doctrinal formulations.

Mary's presence in Scripture was not so completely nonexistent. From the second century, she was described as the new Eve (by Justin and Irenaeus) in a profound and expressive way. As mother of all the living, she is the antitype of Eve, who bound all of humankind by trusting Satan rather than God through the temptations of the flesh and of the spirit. Mary unbound us by consenting to love through her *fiat* (Luke 1:38). Since the middle of the second century, Mary has been beloved by large groups of Christians. The Protoevangelium of James demonstrates the deep trust, tenderness, and love for Mary's zeal, from childhood to the annunciation by the angel (Luke 1:28–38). At three years old, when, as James claims, she herself climbed the steps of the temple, the author writes: "Then she danced and everyone loved her." This is the sign that the author himself and his audience already had a special love for her.

Beginning with the fourth century and most particularly in the fifth and sixth centuries, the nature of the Virgin Mary, Mother of God becomes more evident. Confidence in her mediation increases and is rewarded by the personal and communal favors that she gives so often in a miraculous way. She is commemorated in local liturgies, such as the Feast of the Rosary instituted by Pius V.

The Marian movement (1600–1958), with its tunnel vision and systematic exploitation of *De Maria nunquam satis* ("Of Mary there is never enough"), both in its devotions and its doctrine, was nothing but an extensive overflow of this fervor. Too often, profound and fruitful spiritual intuitions were set aside because this fervor was so demanding and the postconciliar critique was too often contemptuous.

Liturgy is an essential part of the life of the Church. It is what links us to Christ, consciously, visibly, and as a community. It feeds charity and charismatic action in the world, which is in such confusion.

MARY'S INITIAL SILENCE AND HER APPEARANCE IN CHRISTIAN WORSHIP

Mary's presence can only be understood and evaluated genetically. In the beginning, Christian prayer, for which we only have sporadic texts, does not mention Mary. When and how was a place carved out for her, and why was that place so accidental, sporadic, or organic? It is true that, according to Acts 14, Mary was present in the early Church and played a specific role. Her prayer and her memories[1] were influential. But the early kerygma, which centered on the manifestation of Christ from baptism to the resurrection, does not mention her. She is present, like a deep but hidden root. She was not the subject of the Church's preaching.

We cannot ignore the fact that she was the subject of a certain fervor. The Gospel of Luke implies as much: the praise addressed to Mary (Luke 1:28–45) is already in the form of a prayer, which Christians adopted as such from the fourth century. Further, Mary's prediction in the *Magnificat*, "All generations will call me blessed," invites us to praise God himself.

"The disciple took her into his own home" (John 19:27) clarifies the theme of her presence: Mary coming to live with the disciple, the filial piety with which he took her into his home, explains the theme we are exploring. The evangelist speaks about her organic role in the Communion of Saints in John 2:12, in which, after the first "sign," which inspires faith in the disciples, Mary and her family remain with Jesus and his disciples at Capernaum, near Cana. This same reference to the organic place of Mary in the Christian community is explained later in Acts 1:14, where Mary and her family (Jesus' cousins) are assembled with the women to prepare for the Feast of Pentecost.

From the second century, the fervor for Mary is evident in some quarters. She inspired the profuse praise in the Protoevangelium of James that attributes to her all the glories of legal purity (which is a point of contact with the profane for this child, before she is consigned to the holy of holies). When the people see the young Mary dancing for God,[2] "The whole house of Israel loved her." This phrase would be inexplicable if the author and his listeners did not already love Mary. There may be an echo, if not of this fervor, then of admiration in various texts from the second century. This is the case with the *Odes of Solomon*:[3]

> The womb of the Virgin took it, and she received conception and gave birth. So the Virgin became a mother with great mercies. And she labored and bore the Son but without pain, because it did not occur without purpose. And she did not require

a midwife, because He caused her to give life. She brought forth like a strong man with desire, and she bore according to the manifestation, and she acquired according to the Great Power. And she loved with redemption, and guarded with kindness, and declared with grandeur. Hallelujah.

And again this text forms the Sibylline Oracles 8, 456–75 that comments on the annunciation:[4]

First then did Gabriel show
His strong pure form; and bearing his own news
He next addressed the maiden with his voice:
"O virgin, in thy bosom undefiled
Receive thou God." Thus speaking he inbreathed
God's grace on the sweet maiden; and straightway
Alarm and wonder seized her as she heard,
And she stood trembling; and her mind was wild
With flutter of excitement while at heart
She quivered at the unlooked-for things she heard.
But she again was gladdened and her heart
Was cheered by the voice, and the maiden laughed
And her cheek reddened with a sense of joy,
And spell-bound was her heart with sense of shame.
And confidence came to her. And the Word
Flew into the womb, and in course of time
Having become flesh and endued with life
Was made a human form and came to be
A boy distinguished by his virgin birth;
For this was a great wonder to mankind,
But it was no great wonder unto God
The Father, nor was it to God the Son.
And the glad earth received the new born babe,
The heavenly throne laughed and the world rejoiced.

(These texts are often related to the time of Marcus Aurelius.) The prayer and experience of Christians merely express, in the Church, the biblical characteristics present in previous periods. Let us try to understand how and when Mary appeared in Christian worship.

We will avoid the anachronistic, and in many ways regrettable, expression "Marian devotion." Paul VI may have used the phrase (*cultus Marianis*), but he took care not to use it except in correcting a false impression and reminding the faithful that there was a Christian devotion. Mary forms an integral part of it and is not subject to separate or independent devotion. We can recall several corrective statements made by Paul VI:

> Devotion to the Blessed Virgin Mary…forms a very noble part of the whole sphere of that sacred worship.[5]

> Devotion to the Blessed Virgin Mary…fits into the only worship that is rightly called "Christian," because it takes its origin and effectiveness from Christ.[6]

Mary is not subject to separate or independent devotion. In order to help understand this correctly and use the correct terminology, we should not say "Marian dogma"; nor should we use the term *Marian worship*. Therefore what we can say about the presence of Mary is that it is:

1. central to Christian worship; to the Mass;
2. within the liturgical cycle (from Christmas to Easter and Pentecost, as we see from the Bible)—this is the source of our prayer to Mary; and
3. within the Proper of Saints that is followed by the Church, then broadly, at the level of personal piety and devotions, in which Mary's presence is abundantly evident.

MARY'S PRESENCE IN THE MASS

From ancient times, Mary has taken her place at the very center of the Mass, in the canon, before the consecration. This is the formula of our first canon, just before the consecration:

> *Communicantes memoriam venerantes, in primis gloriosae Virginis Mariae, matris Dei et Domini nostri Jesu Christi.*

This Roman canon was introduced in Rome under the pontificate of Leo the Great (440–61). Dom Frenaud, a monk from Solesmes, discovered the unknown ancient origins of the first canon and at the same time perceived that it was of eastern origin. Unfortunately, his report to the International Mariological Congress in Lisbon, where we were together, disappeared in the same fatal accident that cut short his life at the height of his liturgical discoveries. But he had shown me his work and commented on it, and I was able to restore most of his report.

But the canon was not originally written in Latin; it was borrowed from the Greek Mass. It is found in the Syriac Anaphora of the Apostles (beginning in the fourth century) published by Raes, and in the Coptic Anaphora of Saint Basil (about the fourth century), published in 1960, as Dom Frenaud has shown. It puts the Virgin Mary in prime place among the apostles in the Communion of Saints "united in communion." The Virgin, who is the sole author of Christ's human body, and of his human destiny, is commemorated at length, immediately after the first words: "*Communicantes....*" This word is borrowed from Saint Paul (Rom 12:13, in reference to a collection taken from the churches to replenish the resources of the struggling community in Jerusalem) and is used to designate the active communion of churches in the Roman Empire:

oikoumene, which means "the whole inhabited world," from which we get our term *ecumenism*. Saint Basil's wording clearly refers back to this text, which is treated like a prescription by the Apostle:

> This is the precept of the Lord to commune with the memory of the saints (*ut communicamus memoriae sanctorum*).

The liturgy has transformed its meaning. In Rom 12:13, Paul's instructions are to "contribute to the needs of the saints," through the collection. Why, then, does the anaphora speak of communicating with the memory of the (dead) saints? This is due to the similarity of written forms:

> *Mneiais* = remembrance, memory.
> *Xreiais* = necessity, need.
> Optatus of Milevis[7] reads, "*Communicantes memoriis sanctorum*," where the Vulgate actually says, "*Necessitatibus sanctorum communicantes*." Saint Basil[8] also reads the text like that.

The reference to the Communion of Saints, which we already understand to mean the saints in heaven (not just those on earth, as in Paul), changes the meaning and the mention of Mary. She has an important place in the very heart of the Mass, in that she introduces and anticipates, just as in her role at the annunciation and elsewhere.

Before Vatican II, Mary appeared four times in the course of each Mass:

1. In the *Confiteor* (she is still mentioned in one of the three penitential formulas in the current Mass).
2. At the offertory, in the final trinitarian prayer, "Receive, O holy Trinity, this oblation which we make to Thee...in honor of Blessed Mary, ever Virgin, blessed John the Baptist," and so on.

3. In the *Communicantes* (still preserved in Canon I).
4. In the prayer that begins *Libera nos* in which reference to her was removed: "*Libera nos, quaesumus, Domine, ab omnibus malis, praeteritis praesentibus, et futuris: et intercedente beata, et gloriosa semper Virgine Dei Genitrice Maria cum beatis Apostolis tuis Petro et Paulo.*"[9]

Mary's place has therefore been restricted in the postconciliar liturgy.

At least the principal reference to Mary in the canon was retained in the Roman Mass (the Holy Office and Cardinal Ottaviani rigorously protected it from modification). In the eastern liturgy, the invocation of Mary is fostered to a greater extent; a certain number of oblates (patrons) are named in her honor, and she ranks first among those who are saints. Mary maintains her place in the three canons of the Roman Mass. And it is good to make ourselves aware of the other signs of her presence.

MARY'S PRESENCE IN LITURGICAL HISTORY

The most ancient appearance of Mary in worship is at Christmas. This feast was instituted in Rome at the end of the third century and focuses on the historical birth of Christ. This is how Mary first came to be in the liturgy. Homilies and liturgical rites explain her role. The Virgin Mary is, then, perceived as the specific sign of the incarnation of the Son of God: Christ became something that he was not (a man), without ceasing to be what he was (God). Similarly, Mary became what she was not (a mother), without ceasing to be what she was (a virgin).

The eastern Feast of the Epiphany, which is slightly older than Christmas (second century), is attested first by the Gnostics, for whom Christ appeared suddenly at his baptism without any earthly antecedents.[10] According to them, Mary has no place, and she would not have since the festival focuses on the event of Jesus' baptism. In Jerusalem, at the time of Egeria's[11] pilgrimage, this feast centered on the birth of Christ and included an evening celebration in Bethlehem. Jesus' mother therefore formed part of the feast, but we do not know when or how. In Jerusalem, it is only at the end of the fourth century, after the Feast of Christmas had been adopted, that the commemoration of Christ's baptism took place in the celebration of the Epiphany.

In Cappadocia, the Feast of Christmas was celebrated from the year 375, and one of Saint Basil's homilies states that there was a reading from the prophet Isaiah (7:14) about the virgin who would conceive and from the Gospel of Matthew (1:18–25; 2:1–12), where Mary is mentioned at greater length than in Luke.

In the second half of the fourth century, a commemoration of Mary appeared in the East, around the Feast of Christmas. The story of the annunciation was read from the Gospel. For a long time homilies focusing on this celebration were centered on the Feast of the Annunciation, which predated it for this reason. D. Montagna has identified the liturgical function of these homilies, and by doing so has clarified both their meaning and their date. The two oldest homilies known are attributed to Gregory of Nyssa and can be located at the start of the third quarter of the fourth century. They were perhaps responsible for prayer to Mary. In any case, this is the oldest known example of which we can be sure. In the first homily, delivered at Caesarea in Cappadocia between 370 and 378, Gregory of Nyssa, to whom the manuscript tradition attributes the homily, makes this comment:[12]

> Let us proclaim in a loud voice, in keeping with the words of the angel: Rejoice, highly-favored of God, the Lord is with you...

> From you comes him who is perfect in dignity and in
> whom resides the fullness of Godhead.
> Rejoice, beloved of God, the Lord is with you: with the
> handmaid [Luke 1:38] is the King;
> With the immaculate, him who sanctifies the universe,
> With the Fair One, is the fairest of the children of men, to
> save man made in his image.

In the other homily, on the same celebration, Gregory expands his commentary to include the words "You are blessed among women," the words of Elizabeth in Luke 1:42, which some manuscripts also attribute to the angel at the annunciation in Luke 1:28:

> You are blessed among women
> Because among all virgins you were chosen; because you
> were judged worthy to host such a Lord;
> Because you have welcomed Him who fills all…; because
> you have become the spiritual Pearl of great price.[13]

Mary also has a place in feasts relating to the infancy of Christ inspired by the same Gospel. Over and above Mary's place in the context of the Feast of Christmas, which has very different forms in the East and West, the evangelical feasts must be added in which Mary takes her place in the mystery of Christ. First, The Presentation of Jesus at the Temple (the feast commemorating Christ's meeting with Simeon in Luke 2:22–35), which is attested from the end of the fourth century (it became the Feast of the Purification or Presentation or Candlemas), celebrates or "summarizes the whole Mystery of the Incarnation," according to Hesychius.[14] Second, the Annunciation (March 25) is, like the Presentation, a christological feast, but the Virgin Mary takes greater prominence. The Annunciation existed as a feast only from the sixth or seventh century. We have already mentioned previous homilies referring to this commemoration. And finally, the Visitation (which has been transferred from July 2 to May 31) is much more recent. It is unknown in the East and was inaugurated in Prague in 1386, by Archbishop Jean Jenstejn (1348–1400) and spread quickly in the West.[15] Luther was a fervent supporter of this feast and often preached about it and referred to it. However, let us not forget that the Visitation was very ancient in the Latin Church and was the focus of the four weeks of Advent, such that it became a double feast.

PRAYER TO SAINTS AND THE SANCTORAL CALENDAR

Christian worship focuses first of all on Christ alone. But, from the second century, the martyrs also have had a place in worship because their sacrifice and their deaths were a continuation of Christ's passion in his body, the Church. The bodies of the martyrs were collected, buried, and honored. The day of their birth in heaven was celebrated (*dies natalis*). It was only later, in the fourth century, that confessors (ascetics) and Mary herself featured in Christian worship. The day of their death then became their *dies natalis*. It was only then that questions were raised about Mary's *dies natalis*. In 377, Saint Epiphanius investigated this and found that no one knew anything about it: whether she died, or was even still alive, whether she was buried or not, whether she died a martyr's death (which could be one interpretation of Simeon's prophecy in Luke 2:35), or whether she had been taken up to heaven alive, according to one reading of Revelation 12:14.[16] The Apocrypha (which Epiphanius perhaps wished to ignore, if they existed at all at that time), provided a ready response, but with fictional and mythological overtones, and without official credibility.

In Jerusalem, from the beginning of the fifth century, August 15 began to be celebrated as the *dies natalis* of

Mary. This has always been the date on which the Feast of the Assumption has been celebrated. But this celebration had different names:

- Dormition (*Koimêsis*);
- Assumption (*Analêpsis*), which was already celebrated in the second half of the sixth century, according to Theoteknos of Kivias); and
- *Transitus* (passage: *metastasis*; the name also refers to the Apocrypha of the Assumption).

This feast contrasts with saints' feasts by its reference to the Assumption (it is perceived very differently by the Apocrypha, but this will be covered elsewhere, where we give a summary of its theological foundations). It is on the topic of this feast that we find the first explicit developments on Mary's presence.

Other personal feasts of the *Theotokos* soon gather round this feast. They are all inspired by the Protoevangelium of James, an apocryphal infancy narrative written in the second century. The Conception of Mary (end of the seventeenth century) was created following the model of the Feasts of the Conception of John the Baptist and of Christ (the Annunciation). The Nativity of Mary appears to follow the model of the nativities also of Christ and John the Baptist, but, unlike them, on spurious grounds. And the Presentation of Mary in the Temple was another echo of the Protoevangelium of James and its iconography. This feast apparently dates back to the sixth century. All these feasts would be taken on by the Roman world in the course of the seventh century: the Presentation in the Temple (fixed as February 2 around 650), the Dormition, and Annunciation, then the Nativity of Mary (September 8) a little before the end of the seventh century, etcetera.

From the Middle Ages through the modern age, a number of other feasts were established, often linked with particular places. They became so numerous that in the

Breviarium Marianum,[17] there is one for every day of the year, apart from forty-five exceptions, including the Holy Hair (March 8), the Holy Uterus (December 20), the Holy Ring (December 21), and the Incomprehensibility of Mary (December 29). From the seventeenth century, when creativity over Marian devotion in the liturgy was considerable, Rome reacted against the multiplication of feasts. It is under this return to simplicity that Pius X began reducing them.

After the postconciliar reform of 1967, the Commission completely revised the liturgical books. Three feasts disappeared—The Transfixion on Friday of the Passion (which duplicated the feast day on September 15), Our Lady of Mercy (September 24), and the Holy Name of Mary (this was as a result of a *motu proprio* by John XXIII) before the Second Vatican Council on July 25, 1960. Mary, Mother of God was transferred to January 1. And two Marian feast days reverted to feasts of Christ: The Purification of Mary became the Presentation of the Lord in the Temple (February 2), and the Annunciation to Mary became the Annunciation of the Lord (March 25).

So thirteen celebrations remain, of which only five are feast days:

> Three solemnities: Mary, the Mother of God, the Immaculate Conception, and the Assumption.
>
> Two feasts: the Nativity and the Visitation (which was transferred from July 2 to May 31, to come before the Nativity of John the Baptist celebrated on June 24).
>
> Four mandatory memorials: The Queenship of the Blessed Virgin Mary (August 22), Our Lady of Sorrows (September 15), Our Lady of the Rosary (October 7), and the Presentation of the Blessed Virgin Mary (November 21).
>
> Four optional memorials: Our Lady of Lourdes (February 11), Our Lady of Mount Carmel (July

16), the Dedication of the Basilica of Saint Mary Major (August 5), and the Immaculate Heart of Mary (the Saturday after the Feast of the Sacred Heart of Jesus).

PRAYER ADDRESSED TO MARY IN THE LITURGY AND IN THE PRAYER OF THE CHURCH

When did people start praying to Mary? First of all, it is important to distinguish between two things: including Mary in prayer and addressing her directly. *Including Mary in prayer* was the only form that existed in the Roman world until the beginning of the fifth century. The norm of *lex orandi* was that all prayer was addressed to the Father through Christ. And this form is the only one that is admissible, even today, in the canons and the prayers of the Mass. Prayers addressed directly to Christ are rare and relatively recent. They have not been retained in the reformed liturgy.

Mary is not entirely absent from the *lex orandi*; like the saints, she appeared as a motif in prayer, which is always the case in the prayers of the Mass, for example:

> O God, who wished that at the word of the angel, your Word would become incarnate in the womb of the Blessed Virgin Mary, grant the prayer of your servants, that we who truly believe her to be the Mother of God, may be rescued through the grace of her intercession, through the same Jesus Christ our Lord.

God is the only interlocutor, but Mary is present.

Saint Augustine knew only this form of prayer and Protestants accept it. In order for ecumenism to remain healthy, it is good to know that this is a standard form of prayer in the Church that forms a permanent part of the life of the Church. This was an excellent basis for dialogue on the ecumenical text of the Marian Congress of Zaragoza, in 1979.[18]

When and how did *prayer to Mary* come about? We have already seen how the celebration of Mary around Christmas gave an opportunity for preachers to transform the annunciation in Luke 1:28, "Rejoice," and Elizabeth's exclamation, "Blessed are you among women," into a prayer addressed by the liturgical assembly to Mary. These texts, then, attest that prayer to Mary began in the East not much later than 378.

Of course, private prayer could well have been common before these witnesses. Some graffiti found in Nazareth in which Mary was honored very early on have been thought to date from the second or third century, but we must be very careful about the dating of such entries. The most ancient prayer could be the *Sub Tuum Praesidium* preserved in papyrus no. 470 of the John Rylands library.[19] The word *Theotokos* is perfectly legible on an edge of this tattered papyrus. Mercenier dated it to the third century. The fact that the word *Theotokos* is present has prompted a number of commentators to suggest a later date: the fourth or fifth century. But the arguments put forward for advancing the date are not very consistent. Even if the word *Theotokos* has not been confirmed with certainty before the beginning of the fourth century, Origen (c. 185–254) had already used this title in his lost commentary on the "Epistle to the Romans, t. 1."[20] There is no reason to doubt this testimony, because the expression *Theotokos* originated in Egypt.

Theotokos is simply a Greek direct translation of the Coptic *masnouti* (*mas* = to bear a child, *nut* = God): God-bearer. This title seems to have been popular from the third century. It is to be hoped that new expertise will allow the dating of the papyrus itself. But the third century seems to me the most likely date for the *Sub Tuum*:

> Beneath thy mercy,
> we take refuge, O Virgin Theotokos [= Mother of God]:
> disdain not our supplications in our distress,
> but deliver us from perils,
> O only pure and blessed one.

It is in the fourth century, in 379, that Gregory Nazianzen mentions a prayer addressed to Mary by a virgin named Justine, asking for protection against persecutors who wanted to rape her.[21]

THE DEVELOPMENT OF SPECIFIC DEVOTIONS

Since the Middle Ages, private devotions have had an important place, insofar as the monastic liturgy no longer spoke the language of the people. Devotions were practiced as a (healthy or unhealthy) way of compensating for that. Specific devotions "derive from the liturgy" and have the purpose of leading (*Manuducant*) people toward it, in keeping with Vatican II.

In 377, Epiphanius of Salamis came down hard on the popular devotion of women offering cakes to Mary. He denounced the offering of a sacrifice to a creature, calling it an act of idolatry. But he seems to be yielding to two tendencies here—heresiology and misogyny—while at the same time giving in to the traditional laudable desire to stay at the forefront of *lex orandi* and to safeguard sobriety.

The mariological treaties often classify these devotions into celebrations of months, weeks, days, and hours. Thus the celebration of the "Month of Mary" began in Egypt during the patristic era, before reappearing in the modern era in the West. Then came the "Month of the

Rosary," with other months dedicated to Saint Joseph (March) and other saints and devotions.

As for weekly celebrations, we find that, from the Carolingian period, Saturdays were set aside in honor of the Virgin Mary.[22] This devotion took its place in the liturgy under the form of the votive Mass as we know it. For days, we have many novenas and other practices; for hours, the Angelus and other prayers or rites not assigned to particular days. To this we can add Mary's patronage of persons, communities, or shrines that favor using the name of Mary. These devotions are evidence of a desire to make Mary omnipresent in this life.

Mary, then, is present at every Mass, in the fabric of the liturgical year (temporal and sanctoral) and throughout the whole life of the Church. This discreet and forceful omnipresence, which permeates both official and private prayer, responds to her presence within Scripture and reminds us that she lives within the Communion of Saints.

If Mary is present in the prayer of the Church in such a strong way, it is for two reasons: First, she is inseparable from Christ, which is implied in her mysteries and in the first achievement of salvation. Second, her prime place in the Body of Christ has been recognized since the fifth century, in the Church Triumphant, and in her close bond with the Church Militant and the Church Suffering, desiring to "do good on earth" through her intercession, her influence, and her presence. Her place in the prayer and daily life of the Church is a second step in establishing her presence; these elements are accepted as a fact by the Church.

III

MARY'S PRESENCE IN LOCAL CHURCHES

Mary's presence is recognized in the history and memory of the churches, in their archaeology, their iconography, their preaching, celebrations, devotions, and so on. These phenomena are infinitely variable from so many different places and centuries. It is enough to mention some of their characteristics.

Mary's patronage, her intercession, and her heavenly presence have been invoked from the earliest times by the churches both at a national and local level. In Constantinople, the liberation of the besieged city is celebrated and attributed to the intervention of Mary. Increasingly, thousands of communities or religious groups have put themselves under her patronage. Between the seventeenth and the nineteenth centuries this phenomenon was most intense, and it continues. The first feminist group in the USSR, founded by young women who had been brought up in atheism and then converted as a reaction against it, took Mary as its patron, help, and model. Choosing the name Mary means identification, imitation, belonging (*totus tuus*), patronage, and protection. She is present through her memorials in the history of countless churches.

ICONOGRAPHY

Her image came to the fore very early. We first find representations of her in the catacombs, and she holds a place at the forefront of Christian iconography. This is very apt for our purposes, since the icon is a sign of her presence. An icon is not, as in classical painting, a window opened onto an illusory appearance of reality, but more like radiance coming from an active and mysterious space. An icon is less a representation of an object than a sign of transparency. While classical painting attempts to give the illusion of depth by using perspective to deceive the eye, the icon's line of perspective is focused on the one who prays before it. Perspective is reversed. The icon is not so much an object that enters the visual field of the viewer as it is the viewer who is caught in the orbit of the icon, and caught up into that other world. It is not the believer who looks at the icon, so much as the icon that looks at the believer.

Icons of the Virgin are derived from a few basic types, where she is turned toward her Son, or to God in prayer. This is referred to as an *Orante*. These include:

1. *Theotokos* in majesty on a throne, where she holds her son on her lap on the right hand side. Sometimes this is called *Kyriotissa*.
2. The ancient type of *Orante* was used to paint Mary. This was the ancient *Blachernitissa*, so called because of the Virgin of the church of Blachernae. It indicates her relationship to Christ by showing him on his mother's lap.

The other types of representations of the Virgin with her child include most notably the *Hodigitria*: the guide. This name was given to the so-called Virgin of Saint Luke. The prototype can be found in the church of the Hodiges (southeast of Saint Sophia in Constantinople).

Examples of maternal tenderness take various forms:

1. The *Eleoussa*: where the child is held tight against his mother, cheek to cheek (which is derived from the *Hodigitria*)
2. The *Glycophilousa*: kissing the child's hands
3. The *Galactotrephousa*: breastfeeding (this is a later type)

Theology is generally expressed less deeply in icons than in words, but sometimes it is more profound, and appeals to a wider population. It is very important to understand the life of the churches of the past, but also of today, when there is such a dearth of iconography. The iconography of Mary far surpasses, both quantitatively and certainly qualitatively, that of all other saints. The only icons that go beyond hers are those of Christ (in which she is also included).

Some cathedrals, such as Chartres, are "Bibles in stone" and "Bibles in glass" (portals and windows). They make real the Bible and its message: figures and symbols from the litanies to Mary, Gospel scenes in which she plays a role, from the annunciation to the cross and Pentecost, the assumption and the coronation, all of which have sometimes given rise to wonderful iconography.

Shrines are of particular importance. The reason why they have so often and so early been dedicated to Mary is because she was the first shrine of Christ (the first ark of the covenant according to the midrashic symbolism of Luke 1:35, referring back to Exod 40:35). In this respect, she is the prototype for all Christians called to become the temple of God—a living temple, as the Greek Fathers would say. The temple is not a kind of magical place, but a place of prayer. It is a type both of the Church—the Body of Christ—and of the Church as a sanctuary for bringing together Christians. From the fifth century, Proclus of Constantinople considered it as a place for "bringing together and assembling the People of God" for celebrations.[1]

Churches emerged from the third century onward to house large communities that could no longer meet in people's homes; with the conversion of Constantine and the end of the persecution, these became the normal place for holding the liturgy. Earlier basilicas were sporadic or existed only in times and places of tolerance. From the fifth century, Mary's presence is expressed in churches that were dedicated to her. Saint Mary Major, *Salus populi romani*, which was built in the fifth century, was a great comfort for Rome during times of distress; this was the case especially during the Second World War (1940).

In Poland, the church of Our Lady of Czestochowa is built around an icon that is unveiled every afternoon to the sound of the trumpet, in an impressive ceremony that celebrates her presence that is still alive and victorious; it is a memorial of deliverance. Our Lady of Czestochowa has become the national shrine, because the people's prayer was heard when they were being threatened by their enemies. It was at Czestochowa that the famous joint invasion of the Cossacks, Turks, and Swedes took place (1648). Czestochowa was the last stand of resistance: "We will destroy this chicken coop in three days," said the general Burchard as he besieged the last bastion. The siege lasted forty days and failed due to an uprising among the Polish people.

Mary's presence as a sign of hope has taken on an ever-increasing place of importance in the history of this martyred people, who have been so often annihilated. Czestochowa is the icon and the wellspring of all these resistance and resurgence events. At each stage of Polish history this national symbol has grown, most recently with Cardinal Wyszynski's successful resistance against communism and the election of the first Polish pope, whose motto is a symbol of dedication to her: *Totus Tuus*. There are few shrines of such importance for the local church across the nation. It is a fundamental part of the national consciousness in Poland.

France shares the presence of the Virgin among its many cathedrals—Paris, Chartres, and others—and its shrines. This includes Lourdes, which quickly became an important destination for pilgrims after the occurrence of the apparitions in 1858. It is growing ever more important because it is a welcoming place that is well organized and at the same time acts as a symbol. This is the only place capable of hosting the Episcopal Conference or the great pilgrimages (almost 100,000 people take part), where the pilgrims seem almost like prisoners returning from captivity. As of the twenty-first century, five million pilgrims visit Lourdes every year.

Of all the shrines that represent a local church, Our Lady of Guadalupe in Mexico is of the highest importance. It is not just the National Shrine of Mexico, which the bloody persecutions of the anticlerical revolution dared not close. But it is, more and more, becoming the shrine of the continent, a symbol of the new Church among the new peoples of the American hemisphere. We have been very aware in recent years that in Latin America, Christianity has been a colonial import linked to a deadly war that enslaved the Indians. Catholic worship was established first in the cities founded by the *conquistadores*. What is new and revolutionary about the apparition at Guadalupe is that the Virgin appeared, not in the Christian citadels, but among the Indians. Moreover, it was in the place where they worshipped the goddess Tonantzin. Mary visited the poor and oppressed. It was not a bishop who decided to build a church among the Indians in order to Christianize them. Instead, it was an Indian who conveyed to the bishop the order to build a church among them. In some ways, the Indian Juan Diego was the Virgin's plenipotentiary whom the bishop obeyed. The Virgin came down to earth and appeared among the people, thanks to the charisms of the Indian Juan Diego.

In Portugal, the apparitions in 1917 made Fatima a regional shrine that was even more popular and representative for the nation than Lourdes was in France. In France things are more spread out, because there are quite a number of prestigious shrines to the Virgin Mary: Le Puy (since the High Middle Ages), the cathedrals, which we have already mentioned, and the great local shrines, such as Our Lady of Fourvière (Lyon) and Our Lady of Garde (Marseille). But also Valenciennes, where the Virgin's local presence and influence are significant. There are also shrines set up to commemorate apparitions, including the Bac road (1830), La Salette (the apparition of September 18, 1846), Lourdes (1858), and Pontmain (1871). These apparitions serve to remind us that the Virgin Mary is present, protecting us, but they also invite us to live according to Christ's command; to take seriously Mary's injunction to "do whatever he tells you" (John 2:6).

Some other characteristics of the apparitions: in general, they are addressed to the people, to the poor, the recipients of the Gospel, whose prayer and spontaneous activity often establish pilgrimages and shrines before the ever-prudent official Church recognizes them. However, prolonged refusal to acknowledge these phenomena may create uncontrollable tensions between the people and Church authorities. During the middle part of the twentieth century, the suppression of these phenomena became so systematically intransigent that it often resulted in painful and fruitless conflict. In more than one case, it would have seemed wiser to have corrected this situation by channeling the prayer that emerged on the scene of the alleged apparitions. When the people are dissuaded from trusting in these signs by pastoral actions that are often too abstract, they tend to go to the other extreme with regard to the apparitions. It is dangerous to suppress something if you do not know how to give the people more suitable food. The function of these supernatural phenomena (apparitions, charisms) can be compared to that of alcohol: it is a stimulant that calls for moderation. However, alcohol can be a source of nourishment. A laboratory test encapsulates the problem like a parable. Mice that are fed in a normal way do not drink alcohol if you put it in their cage. If they are undernourished, they will. The apparitions are a spiritual stimulant that targets sensitive faculties. This feature has its own ambiguities: "Blessed are those who have not seen and yet have believed," Christ said (John 20:29). Some Christians have a kind of spiritual gluttony and have a taste only for what can be seen and felt, and they forget how to rely on faith. Even at Lourdes, after the authentic apparitions to Bernadette, there was an epidemic of visionaries for months afterward. The bishop suppressed them with good reason, but was also able to recognize Bernadette's as authentic, after mature consideration.

However, if we systematically remove any stimulants or charisms, we end up with a Church that is sleepy, gloomy, and sluggish. Exceptional graces call for discernment, and especially education, so that authentic apparitions may be identified, and suspicious apparitions may be channeled into an authentic prayer life. The best outcome is to educate rather than repress, which is a solution that is required only in extreme cases.

Apparitions often spark lively enthusiasm among the people, and spontaneous worship, which the clerical hierarchy tends to oppose. At Lourdes, for example, Bernadette, the visionary, was a poor little girl. Her family was ruined and despised. The apparitions of the Virgin are a sign, like the light set on a lampstand mentioned in the Gospel parable (Matt 5). The apparitions that happened during the two weeks between February 11 and March 4, 1858, caused a group to gather, and then a crowd. People came earlier and earlier to find a good spot for the morning apparitions. They revived the Christian tradition of prayer vigils. For a long time, the ecclesiastical authority remained cautious and suspicious. It was this popular initiative that created the first prayer traditions of Lourdes and that gave the first offerings where "the greatest riches came from the poorest people" as the surprised and somewhat shocked police commissioner pointed out. Ropes were installed all the way down to the cave, along the steep slope. Plumbers installed the first three spigot basins to collect water from the fountain and allow people to wash there. It was only after nine months that the pilgrimage was subjected to episcopal investigation. It was gradually taken in hand by the authorities, who took over, recognizing the authenticity of the apparitions four years later (on January 18, 1862).

THE CONCILIAR MEANING OF THE LOCAL CHURCHES

It is important to locate Mary's presence at the level of the local church, because it is at this level that the Church exists most fully.

This may seem self-evident, but the Church is not a general phenomenon. We cannot look at it the way we would look at, say, a map of the Roman Empire. The Church is local in character, and is established in a certain city or environment, as the first missionaries, Paul and Barnabas, intended. Each church comes into being in accordance with the language and culture of its own place. It finds full life through the Word, the Eucharist, and the bishop, who is a sign of unity and of the authority of Christ. If the Church is alive and well grounded, it will spread, as did the church at Antioch (Acts 13), and churches in their turn will arise in other places. From within they form their ministers, their places of worship, their icons, depending on the language and culture, the style and temperament of each place. Normally this results in differentiation, which enriches unity in the body. The universal Church is a gathering together of all these basic living entities. Their unity lies in the fact that they come from the same source: the Gospel and the Holy Spirit who gives them life within the heart of them. So, this unity is, above all, an internal and living thing. It is the convergence of a single purpose: returning to the Father through Christ. The service of the people and the Church is fruit of that. That is what keeps the Church free from centralization and dictatorship, despite some traditions of possessiveness inherited from Roman imperialism, which the Council has reduced by defining the extent of the bishops' powers and the scope of local churches; Paul VI implemented this at the request of the Council.

THE WITNESS OF THE LOCAL CHURCHES: DIVERSITY IN UNITY

The richness of local churches is inexhaustible. Let us be clear here; as we indicated in previous chapters, Vatican II laid emphasis on local churches in order to address a rigid structure in which the Roman Church was the concrete, pervasive, and all-embracing measure of all others. The Council proclaimed:

> Within the Church particular Churches hold a rightful place; these Churches retain their own traditions, without in any way opposing the primacy of the Chair of Peter, which presides over the whole assembly of charity and protects legitimate differences, while at the same time assuring that such differences do not hinder unity but rather contribute toward it (*Lumen Gentium* 2).

So we move from a model of uniformity to one of differentiation in unity, which corresponds to the function of the Holy Spirit in the Church: to awaken every Christian and every community to their unique identity, to their diversity in unity.

This theology of the individual church revives the words of Saint Paul (Rom 16:5; 1 Cor 16:9; Col 4:15). Repercussions of it were felt throughout the work of the Council. Using this as its basis, the Decree on Ecumenism recognized some communities that were separate as churches. The reality of the individual churches regained its consistency and force in the decrees on bishops (No. 6, 16, 19, 22, 27), which establishes decentralization without disintegration.

The place of Mary in local churches shows us in a striking way the unity in diversity that characterizes the Church. Diversity has a dual purpose:

1. The cultural foundation of each church; hence, the iconography and different architecture that also emerge in certain periods.
2. The working of the Holy Spirit, who awakens every Christian and every community to their freedom, therefore to their diversity, according to their roots— there are, for example, representations of the Virgin Mary as black or blonde according to the different types of iconography.

So it is also with architecture, the plastic arts, and local practices with regard to devotion to Mary; these illustrate the infinite variety in the theology of local churches.

So here we find two aspects of Mary's presence: (1) The free gift of God, including exceptional signs such as the apparitions, and (2) The mobilization of the people of God, directed by pastoral authority. Manifestations of piety toward Mary could be classified as coming from these two sources.

Mary takes up such a visible, and often radiant or moving, role in local churches because she herself is a sign (Isa 7:14; Rev 12:1). She still manifests herself as a sign of God's mercy; and the churches like to illustrate this sign fervently. There is nothing abstract about her presence.

Let us therefore remember this third milestone—the life and vitality of local churches—and the diversity in unity they show: "*Vestis circundate varietate aurea*" ("her clothing is inwrought with varieties of gold"), as the poetic language of the psalm conveys. It remains to be seen how we are made aware of Mary's presence in the interior and mystical life of the churches.

IV

WITNESSES IN TRADITION

The previous chapters, and what we have examined so far, have centered around the word *presence*. Here we aim to extend the search to other more or less equivalent expressions, because it is important to delve into the sources of this significant experience of a remarkable aspect of the Christian life.

We reach this ineffable and often silent experience through limited expressions, some of which may be insufficient or overblown. They can often be refracted through the ideas or theories of the person who describes them. We should be wary of ideologies, superstructures, and superfluities; be on the lookout for mismatches; and be aware of the diversity of the aforementioned experiences and expressions. We are not trying to promote an experience of Mary that combines all the traits expressed by various mystics. When we first become aware of her presence, we find particular graces that are specific, exceptional, and of the moment. So at each stage we should ask ourselves whether we are dealing with an ordinary or extraordinary experience. Is it normal or exceptional? Passing or permanent?

So this stage has a double function: information and evaluation with discernment. First, we collect the scattered evidence on the presence of Mary, expressed over the centuries, in chronological order. And second, we evaluate the nature, characteristics, and the fruits of the experience—distinguishing the essence of the diverse and accidental forms—by discerning the ordinary from the extraordinary and the normal from the pathological, because it is important not to confuse the authentic presence of Mary with excrescences and distortions. Mainly, we need to ask ourselves: Is it a gift or the result of an effort of asceticism? Does this form of piety fit all or is it restricted? Where does this presence come from? And how are we made aware of it?

A BIBLICAL YARDSTICK

In Scripture, the only evidence of the theme of Mary's presence, as some Christians live it today, is John 19:27: "The disciple took her into his own home." Many followers since then have taken Mary into their homes. In some sense, she lives with them.

We have seen that Mary's living with the disciple is symmetrical to her living with Jesus' brothers, his disciples, and Jesus himself, after Cana in John 2:12. This verse foreshadows Mary's living with the "brothers" and the "disciples" (Acts 1:14) in the primitive community, waiting for the Holy Spirit in prayer and in koinonia ("communion"). Mary's presence at the birth of the Church corresponds to her presence at the birth of Christ, in both cases under the sign of the Holy Spirit (Luke 1:35; Acts 1:8). This information gleaned from Scripture is implicit, but of great objective importance, both materially and spiritually, and rich in suggestion.

Saint Ambrose of Milan touches upon Mary's presence when commenting on the visitation, the fruitful meeting of Mary and Elizabeth, of Christ and John the Baptist (see below). Here we are dealing with the presence of Christ and Mary with John the Baptist, at the visitation. But these mysteries have, for Ambrose, a certain continuity, a typical, symbolic, and permanent value that the following explains more fully:

It must be the soul who receives the Word: she died to the world and is buried with Christ. All this, taken together, means that Mary is a type of the Church and of the Christian soul and Jesus is a sign [*signaculum*] established in Mary; and Mary is a sign of Christ, by her faith and her virginity which give birth to Christ.[1]

THE PATRISTIC PERIOD (SECOND TO EIGHTH CENTURIES)

There are very few texts on Mary dating from the second century. It is debatable whether she had a place in the liturgical and spiritual life of the first Christians. For this period (second and third centuries), there are only a few texts on Mary, especially since the liturgy was improvised and was passed on through oral tradition.

THE PROTOEVANGELIUM OF JAMES (CA. 150)

However, the Protoevangelium of James shows that the Virgin Mary was already present in the Christian imagination in popular piety. When telling us about Mary in the Temple, Pseudo-James writes, "Mary danced and everyone loved her." The testimony of this apocryphal work has long been ignored as being without historical value, but it does tell us the place that the Virgin Mary held in Christian life and in the hearts of the faithful at the time. The person who wrote it already loved Mary and addresses himself to Christians who also love her and are eager to know more about her from her infancy. She was present following the Gospel, which this ancient text uses and extends. The word *presence* appears from the third century on but without its true meaning being explained.

ORIGEN (DIED CA. 254)

In his commentary on the visitation, Origen thinks that the presence of both Mary and Jesus must have had an effect on Elizabeth and her son: "It is inconceivable that in three months, in the presence of the Mother of the Lord and the Savior himself, Elizabeth and John did not make progress [spiritually]." In the light of what is reported in the Gospel, from the beginning of Mary's greeting, her cousin Elizabeth is filled with the Holy Spirit (Luke 1:41), at the same moment as her son, who leaps for joy (Luke 1:15).

EPHREM (DIED 373)

The Syrian deacon Ephrem lived and taught about his trust in the presence of Mary. He bases his confidence on her special title of Mother of God and the corresponding grace of being not only a guide but a "refuge, protection, and defense." He does not speak explicitly of the motherhood of Mary with regard to humanity (which is so little documented in the East) but of her implicit presence, because the final image is of a mother who takes her children "by the hand" and leads them to eternal life. This text, whose authenticity is better attested, is full of strong and tangible conviction: "You, Our Lady, Virgin and Mother, take care of me through the purity of your divine grace, guide my life and show me the way to the holy will of your Son. Give me pardon for my sins, be my refuge, protection and defense; take me by the hand and lead me to eternal life."[2]

AMBROSE OF MILAN (DIED 397)

It is also the visitation that inspires in Ambrose of Milan the same way of describing the influence of Mary: "The greater comes to the aid of the lesser: Mary to Elizabeth, Jesus to John...and we immediately see the benefits of the presence of Mary and of the Lord."[3] Mary's coming (*adventus*) and the "presence (*praesentia*) of the Lord" are contrasted here (parallel terms used as a cause for blessings). And Ambrose uses the word *presence* for Mary, as he does for Jesus, in another commentary on the visitation: "The presence of the Word imbues the soul with a power like that of the presence of Mary (*praesentia Mariae*), who had Him in her womb, and affects John, in Elizabeth's womb, to the point where he dances and rejoices."[4]

It is in this broad and general sense that the word *presence* emerges here to describe the personal encounter of the two mothers. Ambrose expresses in a poetic way their inseparable gift, which is transferred from the Messiah to his precursor and from Mary to Elizabeth. But in his mind, the gift is shared among them and is unique, it seems.

CHROMATIUS OF AQUILEIA (FIFTH CENTURY)

In the fifth century, Chromatius of Aquileia expressed how important, or necessary, Mary was to the birth of the Communion of Saints by becoming the first member of the Word incarnate. It was about this deep inner sense that he wrote, "We cannot talk about the Church without including Mary, the Mother of the Lord, along with his brothers." He expressed this thought as though it were a reminiscence and even quotes from John 2:12; after the miracle at Cana, Jesus "went down to Capernaum with his mother, his brothers and his disciples, and they stayed a few days." Luke says the same in Acts 1:12–14.

It was a well-established conviction throughout the east, as evidenced by the discovery of the *Sub tuum*, in 1938, among the desert sands of Egypt—a prayer that was thought to be Latin and medieval in origin, but which papyrologists at first dated to the third century. (Nowadays it is thought to date between the third and fourth centuries, for fear of anticipating the Marian devotion already attested to in the Protoevangelium of James.) This ancient prayer harmonizes with the fervent beliefs of Ephrem and attests to its popularity, albeit in different words: "Under the shelter of your mercy we take refuge, *Theotokos*. Do not deny the requests [we make to you] and when we are in trouble, save us from peril, [you who] alone are chaste and blessed."

As with Ephrem, trust is based on Mary's title, *Theotokos*, which is well documented from the fourth century and perhaps already contained in texts by Origen and preserved in Greek literature. But it is also based on her "mercy" (her tenderness of heart) and the blessings that accrue to her because of her freely chosen virginity and chastity. More exactly, Mary is a help in distress, "in trouble" or in difficulties and other dangers of this life, which, in the Middle Ages, was the basis for the excess of devotion to the "Mother of Mercy."

ILDEFONSUS OF TOLEDO (DIED 667)

Saint Ildefonsus of Toledo is the first to devote himself as a spiritual slave to Mary, who called herself a servant of the Lord. He reveled in this demanding maternal servitude because it guides us and shows us Christ, her Son, and the glory of her virginity. Ildefonsus is the source of that medieval fervor and of the theology of the Virgin, which came into being in the eleventh and twelfth centuries throughout the whole of the west, along with Saint Anselm, Saint Bernard, and many others. Already in his own time he expressed profound insight and an awareness of a living and intimate relationship with the Virgin that coincides with those of the eastern witnesses.

> How quickly I aspire to enslave myself to this Lady, how faithfully I relish the yoke of bondage, how I want to be fully in her service, how ardently I asked never to be separated from her power!
>
> But now I come to you, my sole Virgin and Mother of God; I fall on my knees before you,

who alone bore the Incarnation of my God; I humble myself before you, who alone has been called the mother of my Lord; I pray to you, the only one to be called handmaid of your Son, that you wipe out the punishment due for my sins, grant that I may be purified of the evil of my actions, make me love the glory of your virginity...reveal the great sweetness of your Son.[5]

THE BYZANTINE HOMILISTS

JOHN OF THESSALONICA (SEVENTH CENTURY)

Mary gives light and confidence until the "end of time."

GERMANUS OF CONSTANTINOPLE (DIED 733)

Germanus of Constantinople describes an experience that is less personal than ecclesial and communitarian in his first homily on the Dormition:

You who fully lived with God, left the world without abandoning those who were in the world....We have the custom of venerating with faith...we called them thrice blessed those who enjoy your visible presence [*paroikias*, *deoikia*: "house," "dwelling"] as those who know where to find you [literally "to acquire you, obtain you, possess you": the verb *katakataomai*] as mother of life. Indeed as you walk with us bodily, yet the eyes of our spirits are trained [*psychagontai*] each day to see you.

Just as you remained [*sunepoliteou*, from polis: "town, city"] physically with those of the past [cf. John 19; 27; Acts 1; 14], so you live with us in spirit [*pneumatisynoikeis*]. The powerful protection with which you cover us is a sign of your presence [*synomilian*, from *homilia*: "society meeting"] among us. We listen to your voice and our voices reach your ears. We are known to you through your help and we recognize your powerful lasting help. And I say that not even the separation of soul and body may alter the human relationship between you and your servants [*doulôn*]. You did not abandon those you have saved [*diesôsas*]. You have not forsaken those you have gathered, for your spirit lives forever, and your flesh did not see the corruption of the tomb.

You visit all [people] and your eyes [*episkopé*: "vigilance"] are over all, O Mother of God, though our eyes are prevented from seeing you, most holy one! You have sojourned among us all, and you manifest yourself to those who are worthy of you....

Truly, yes truly, I say in thanksgiving, you have not forsaken the Christian people, you have not rejected this corrupt world for incorruptible life, but you are close to those who invoke you.[6]

This text is probably the oldest we have.[7] It expresses Mary's presence with a great wealth of vocabulary on two levels:

1. Dwelling, expressed by the words *paroikias* and *sunoikeis*, which comes from the root *oik*, "to dwell," from which we get the word *oikia*, "house"; *synomilia*, from *homilia* meaning "society, assembly, friendship," which is reinforced by the prefix *syn*, which puts across the idea of "synthesis, meeting, communion" (it is the same prefix as in *synoikeis*). All this is based on Mary's dwelling with God through the assumption (*the first phrase*).

2. On Mary's part, Germanus of Constantinople refers to both her knowledge and her protective gaze (*episkopé*) in clear contrast with our own sight, which is plunged in the darkness of faith: "Although our eyes are prevented from seeing you." But he also means her protection, which covers us (like a cloak?); her influence, which guides and leads us (*psychagontai*); her voice, which gives us counsel; and her help or assistance, which saves us (*diesôsas*): "We are known to you through your help."

However, Germanus's perspective is not that of the bodily and glorious assumption, but rather of a separation of the soul from the body that does not remove Mary, "for your spirit lives forever, and your flesh did not see the corruption of the tomb." But he seems to think, along with other apocryphal writers, that her body remained incorruptible under the tree of life, waiting for the communal resurrection on the Day of Judgment.

On the part of Christians, her presence is meant as reverence and delight. Mary is received, acquired, and possessed as the mother of life. We hear her voice and know it through her help. So, the text indicates that there is a reciprocity involved in this human relationship, living among us, visiting all. This expression is further enhanced by the presence of a series of contrasts: although she left this earth, Mary has not abandoned us (this theme recurs insistently). Even if we cannot see her, she sees us. She has not abandoned this corrupt world, but draws near to us. The richness and abundance of expression in this text are overwhelming.

Semiotically, the coherence of the text can be seen in the contrasted relationship between a double set of conjunctions and disjunctions:

Disjunction: Mary has left the earth.
Conjunction: in order to meet God.

But Mary's separation from the world is not a disjunction for those who "invoke her," "know how to find her," "listen to her voice."

ANDREW OF CRETE (DIED CA. 740)

For Andrew it is through entry into the eternal life of God that Mary's presence becomes universal and clear.

ANONYMOUS AUTHOR FROM THE SEVENTH AND EIGHTH CENTURIES

Although you have left the world, yet the whole world possesses you: everywhere signs of your presence can be seen. No place is deprived of your protection, O glory of believers, O Virgin among mothers.

This text contrasts the bodily absence of Mary in heaven with her universal and beneficent presence guaranteed by the Church. Her protection is an unfailing sign of her real presence. This contrast is classic and underpins the Byzantine homilists.

JOHN OF DAMASCUS (DIED 749)

Saint John of Damascus contrasts Mary's life on earth and in the tomb with her glorious presence in heaven. We must keep the memory of her earthly presence with Christ in order to find this dual reason for hope, because Mary is identified with Christ: it is in him that we will find her. John is constantly delighted by her presence. She is before him night and day. He is telling us about an experience that is both personal and communal. He specifies the nature of the mutual presence in the faith. This realization is an important and very real moment in our lives.

Divine power is not restricted by place, neither is the Mother of God's working. If it were confined to the tomb alone, few would be the richer. Now it is freely distributed [*aphthonôs dianemmêtai*] in all parts of the world. Let us then make our memory serve as a storehouse of God's Mother. How shall this be? She is a virgin and a lover of virginity [*philoparthenos*]. She is pure [*agnê*] and a lover of purity. If we purify our mind [*mnêmên*] with the body, we shall possess her grace [*charin…*]. In a word, she grieves over every sin [*kakiai*], and is glad at all goodness as if it were her own [*oikeios*]. If we turn away from our former sins in all earnestness and love goodness with all our hearts, and make it our constant companion, she will frequently visit her servants [*thamina pros tous oikeious oiketas leucetas*], bringing all blessings with her, Christ her Son, the King and Lord who reigns in our hearts.[8]

The phrase: "Let us then make our memory serve as a storehouse of God's Mother" is an invitation to us to dispose ourselves to welcome her into our memory as a way of growing in the "virtues." That is what will invite Mary to visit us. The deliberate alliteration of *oikeious* and *oiketas*, in which the root *oik* means "dwelling, living," explains well this presence in terms that are unfortunately untranslatable: "Come and inhabit the inhabitants of your virtues" could be a way of rendering this kind of alliteration, or: "Come and dwell in those who have prepared your dwelling by cultivating your memory and your virtues."

Similarly, in his *Sermon 1 on the Assumption*, John of Damascus says:

Thy most precious gift is the cause of our lasting joy. How it fills us with gladness! How the mind that dwells on this holy treasury of Thy grace enriches itself. This is our thank-offering to thee, the first fruits of our discourses, the best homage of my poor mind, whilst I am moved by desire of thee, and full of my own misery. But do thou graciously receive my desire, knowing that it exceeds my power. Watch over us, O Queen, the dwelling-place of our Lord. Lead and govern all our ways as thou wilt. Save us from our sins. Lead us into the calm harbor of the divine will. Make us worthy of future happiness through the sweet and face-to-face vision of the Word made flesh through thee.[9]

In Pseudo-Germanus of Constantinople's sermon *On the Dormition*, just before the assumption the apostles say to Mary, "Go from the body, stay in the Spirit [*synparamene pneumati*] with your serfs and slaves."[10]

MARY'S PRESENCE THROUGH INVOCATION

It is very natural that invoking Mary results in her presence—we can understand this from the sermons on the assumption, which ask the opposite question: How do you remain present with us, even though you have left this world?

However, Mary's current relationship with humanity works in two quite different ways. Most of the texts speak of *intercession*; that is, Mary's intervention in our relation with Christ that manifests itself in the present. Mary prays to him and it is he who acts and hears immediately. If we think of it like this, it is Christ who is our mediator, and Mary's presence may seem remote from his mediation (at least in the way it is carried out). Here we can quote, by way of example, the end of Germanus of Constantinople's first *Sermon on the Assumption*: "Christ has taken you...to enjoy your presence and your tenderness...this is why all that you ask of Him he gives you like a mother attentive to the needs of her children, and all you ask, he accomplishes with divine power."

Intercession and presence are two modes of expression that are quite different or opposite. We can describe intercession as Mary always turning toward Christ, obtaining for us through her intercession the grace that is the immediate gift of Christ. The model of Marian mediation (see further on), where everything passes through Mary, who is located between Christ and us as a channel or aqueduct, tends to represent the presence of Mary as immediate. The unfortunate consequence of this is that Christ seems more distant and remote because of his transcendence. This insistence on the immediate closeness of Mary set up an unfortunate contrast between Christ's mercy and his terrible justice.

The lesson we can draw from this confrontation is that these spatial models are relative and require rectification. The most important thing is to perceive the perfect communion between Mary and Christ: they share everything, immediately, without these relays and intermediaries multiplying their influence over material things.

Those who confine themselves to speaking to Mary as their model make Christ more distant. Others combine this with her active influence. Olier goes so far as to call Mary a sacrament that communicates the life of Jesus. Existentially speaking, we could describe this dynamic as the inner icon of Mary in the Christian soul—Grignion de Monfort refers to this when he says, "I carry her within me, engraved with lines of glory."[11] Analyzing these concepts helps us to locate and interpret the texts from later centuries.[12]

THE MIDDLE AGES (NINTH TO FIFTEENTH CENTURIES)

ALCUIN (DIED 804)

Mary's presence emerges during the Carolingian era in an inscription attributed to Alcuin:

> *Dies nostros precibus rege semper unique*
> *ut nos conservet pia gratia Christi.*
> Guide us always and everywhere by your prayers
> so that the holy grace of Christ will preserve us.[13]

Alcuin, to whom we owe the choice of Saturday, the vigil of the Lord's Day, as the liturgical day of Mary, calls upon Our Lady in the prayer of the Church to "keep us in the presence of Christ." In this way he took care to mark a regular presence of Mary in the liturgy but always in reference to Christ.

RABANUS MAURUS (DIED 856)

He implores "Mary who is present" to help her servants, based on their mutual relationship.

MILO OF SAINT-AMAND (DIED CA. 871)

While admiring her "noble virginity," he invites Mary's help; she whom the Lord, who was incarnated in her, has filled with humility.

GEORGE OF NICOMEDIA (DIED 880)

He completed a remarkably impressive homogeneous work on the Byzantines that was closely inspired by the influence of the *Theotokos*, and incorporated divine transcendence in a radical way. It thus extended Mary's maternal mission in relation to his favorite disciple (John 19:25–26).

RADBOD OF UTRECHT (DIED 918)

He was spoken to by the Virgin. She looked at him and consoled him by her presence because of the diligence of his prayers to God.

ODILO OF CLUNY (DIED 1049)

He implores her as the "very merciful advocate."

ANSELM OF LUCCA (DIED 1086)

He sighed before the "clement presence" of Mary. He begged her in her compassion to look upon her servant and give him the consolation of her love. Like the others, he does not separate the divine transcendence of this presence from its actualization in everyday life.

"CODEX GERTRUDIANUS"

This text contains this prayer to Mary: "Although I am corrupt, you deign to help me."

PETER DAMIAN (DIED 1072)

Along with John of Damascus, Peter Damian links memory and presence. The *Liber salutatorius*, which is attributed to him, says: "Sweet is her memory, sweeter still is her presence."[14]

ANSELM OF CANTERBURY (DIED 1109)

Anselm was the one who, in the twelfth century, inspired fervor that was both penetrating and promotional. He expressed to Mary his filial love and trust.

AMADEUS OF LAUSANNE (DIED 1115)

Amadeus refers to her presence in his sermon *On the Assumption:*[15]

> Therefore let us eagerly celebrate the Mother of life, source of mercy, brimming with delights and leaning on her Beloved.
>
> With a motion like lightning, extending her six-winged seraph's wings, she now enjoys the love of the Deity [*Deitatis amore*] in the source of life. Now lighting up [*illustrans*] the earth with her signs and her virtues, she hastens ahead of us like a very kind and admirable mother. By her presence, she makes some victorious, by dominating their vices, through her holy intervention and puts them in possession of great virtues. For others she opens the gates to intimate contemplation, and to still others, she offers at the end of their lives, a safe path, so that none of the adversary's power can touch those to whom the Mother the Son of God gives access to Christ.[16]

BERNARD OF CLAIRVAUX (DIED 1153)

Mary's presence fills the inhabitants of heaven since she has been physically and visibly taken there. It also fills and illuminates "the entire universe."

ODON OF MORIMOND (DIED 1161)

In a beautiful text on the spiritual maternity that Jesus has entrusted to Mary, he draws conclusions that explicitly involve the presence of Mary. Because of Jesus' words, "Son here is your Mother" (John 19:27), he says: "Do not despise me, holy Mother, I too am your son....I fervently entrust you with myself and all my needs. Today I will choose you, Mother and Patroness, before all and in all. Despise me not O Holy Mother."[17] He draws demanding consequences from his choice and his dedication. Quoting from Grignion of Montfort, he distinguishes true sons from false sons according to their faithfulness to God, to his moral and evangelical requirements.

> Do you want to know who is the true son of the Virgin Mary? It is he who, in addition to totally surrendering of himself ["dedication": *obsequio mancipavit*] to the Virgin, loves God with all his heart, renounces the pleasures of the flesh and gives to whoever is close to him works of mercy as he can. It is surely him of whom Christ says to Mary: "Here is your son (Jn 19:26)."
>
> What do you say now, oh false son of Mary, you who falsely usurp the title of her maternity carrying hatred in your heart and fraud against your neighbor by your tongue, taking pleasure, despite yourself, by neglecting the precepts of God? What do you say? You talk as if the Virgin Mary belonged to you alone. However, she has no relationship with you. Why do you blaspheme, miserable creature, by invoking the mother whose son you fight against? Do you not know that blasphemers should be stoned?[18]

So, Grignion of Montfort was not the one who invented the accusation of blasphemy against presumptuous devotees who try to cover up their sins with the mantel of the Virgin:

> Nothing is so damnable in Christianity than this diabolical presumption, for can one say that one loves her and honors the Holy Virgin when by one's sins one pricks, pierces, crucifies and mer-

cilessly insults Jesus Christ her Son? If Mary performs an act of mercy by saving these kinds of people, she would be allowing the crime to go unpunished, she would be helping to crucify and outrage her Son: who would ever dare to think such a thing?

I say that to abuse the devotion to the Blessed Virgin, which, after devotion to Our Lord in the Blessed Sacrament, is the holiest and most righteous, is to commit a horrible sacrilege, which, after the sacrilege of receiving communion in an unworthy state, is the greatest and least forgivable sin.[19]

Odon of Morimont concludes on the presence of Mary:

As for us, dear brothers, let us be the disciples that Jesus loves standing [near the cross], so that each of us had the good fortune to hear those sweet words of Jesus: Behold your Mother. O word worthy to be received by us! Behold your Mother: love her and venerate her presence everywhere and expect nothing more, but in that time, accept her, so that finally she will bear you up in her glory where she reigns with her Son, who is over all, God blessed for ever and ever. Amen.[20]

ANONYMOUS

An anonymous hymn:

Gaude mea mediatrix	Rejoice my mediatrix
mea sola consolatrix	my only consoler
mea mater et amatrix	my mother and loving one [*amatrix*: "one who loves"]
O felix quen inhabitas	O happy are those who live in you.[21]

ROMAN LITURGY OF THE THIRTEENTH CENTURY

The liturgy of the visitation sees in this mystery the starting point for Mary's visits to her children.

FRANCIS OF ASSISI (DIED 1226)

Like many authors from this time, Francis did not refer to the spiritual maternity of Mary in a specific way (John 19:25–27), but that does not diminish his trust in Mary in the slightest. According to his biography, he put his nascent order under the protection of "her wings."

ANTHONY OF PADUA (DIED 1231)

The most popular Franciscan saint was sensitive to the influence of her presence. He refers to Mary's presence in four sermons that were formally consecrated to Mary. In the final invocation at Notre Dame, he expresses the essence of the doctrine concerning her: "And so we pray to you, Our Lady, our hope, we are shaken by the storm of the sea, Thou Star of the Sea, shine out, lead us to the port, help us to reach shore through your protecting presence."[22]

Here we find the word *presence* prominently placed at the end, but the metaphorical context does little to clarify its meaning.

THOMAS AQUINAS (DIED 1274)

We mention Saint Thomas here not because of formal texts on the presence of Mary, but because he was the first to propose a typology of her presence. The author of the *Summa Theologica* distinguishes real union (presence in a specific place) and "affective" union that makes us desire it.

PETER THOMAS (DIED 1366)

He was the Attorney General of the Carmelites at the papal court at Avignon, and is considered to have paved the way for the mystical Marian presence among the Carmelites.[23] He took the Holy Virgin as his special patron and placed all his trust in her help; she was his "hope, his support and his extraordinary consolation." As the measure of all holiness, she brought Brother Peter to such degrees of grace and perfection that he often experienced the taste of spiritual joys.

In his biography, written by Wadding, we find the following observations:

> He resolved not to lose any opportunity of rendering homage to his Benefactress...whenever he prayed he mixed in prayers of praise to Mary....And food seemed tasteless to him if it was not raised by the thought of Mary....In his fights against the cunning of the enemy, he advanced in such a way that he used the name of Mary as a shield in each battle. This immense fervor of Marian piety so enveloped and animated his affections and thoughts that he seemed to know nothing, to do nothing, see nothing and hear nothing.[24]

JOHN GERSON (DIED 1429)

If Gerson speaks explicitly of Mary's presence, it is in reference to his concern to find her in the Eucharist:

> O Holy Virgin, dare we say that you are here in this church, in your real presence, just as your Son Immanuel is? Yes, you are here. Perhaps not in the body, but with a glorified body, and by using its agility, you are here invisible. At least

you are present in this sanctuary, through a spiritual influence that you deign to exert on those
who love you, and through the sweet looks with
which your eyes are turned down towards us.[25]

Gerson was among those who tried to explain the presence of Mary in the Communion of Saints, in reference to
the Eucharist, the sacrament of the presence of Christ and
his mystical body. However, he makes the necessary distinction: he is not speaking of a bodily presence, but of
influence and action.

THE RENAISSANCE

The Renaissance period (around the fifteenth and sixteenth centuries) seems less likely to evoke the presence
of Mary than was the fervor of the Middle Ages.
Admittedly, her presence is not forgotten but no longer
holds the same place in the profusion of popular devotions, which were cultivated only superficially and were
sometimes based on superstition.

ARNOLD BOST (DIED 1499)

The other predecessor, often quoted in the development of a Marian way of life in the seventeenth century, is
Arnold Bost, another champion of the Immaculate
Conception, who, at the request of his prior, wrote *De
Mariae patronatu in dicatum sibi Carmeli ordinem.* He
showed how "the most holy Patroness of Carmel, Mary,
Mother of God, has often favored his religious family with
special help."[26] His fervor did not lack imagination since,
according to him, "Elijah [the Prophet] was swallowed
whole in the love of the Virgin...and, like those who are in
love, he gave her the gold ring of his faith, as though she
were his wife."

The writings express the feeling of Mary's presence, which involves diligent imitation and constant thought: "O brother, do not let a day go by, nor a night, nor any travel, nor action, nor talk, nor joy, nor sorrow, nor rest, without remembering her loving presence."[27]

IGNATIUS OF LOYOLA (DIED 1556)

In his autobiographical *Spiritual Journal*, Saint Ignatius saw Mary as an integral part of the Eucharist, to the point that he could perceive in an ineffable way how the flesh of Mary is present in the flesh of her Son (which she had given to him). He does not explain this inexpressible intuition further.

THE SEVENTEENTH AND EIGHTEENTH CENTURIES

In the seventeenth century, there are numerous testimonies.

FRANCIS DE SALES (DIED 1622)

Monsignor Francis Vincent quotes this line from Francis de Sales: "Whenever I enter a place devoted to this august Queen, I feel a certain thrill in my heart, knowing I am in my mother's house."[28]

I could not find this text, even with the help of the most skilled editor, Father Ravier. This is probably because it is reported by some biographer, and Archbishop Vincent unfortunately does not give the reference. I did not find it in Flachaire. But this sentiment fits in well with the experience and doctrine of Francis de Sales, which says in part, "Let us hold fast to God and to the Holy Mother."[29]

Father Ravier sent me this note by Francis de Sales for a sermon on the *Angelic Salutation* (1595): "[Heretics] argue that [those whom Paul greeted] were present through his letter and message, but Our Lady is present among Christians through her care."

JEAN-JACQUES OLIER (DIED 1657)

On one particular Saturday, Olier, who often insisted that the Virgin was present wherever there was a statue or some other sign in the street, saw Mary internally as a "sacrament" by which she communicates the life of her son. These signs are identified with her, in God (John 17:21–22): "She reminded me that her dear Son told me that he would live in me only in her and through her, and with the life he lived in her, as if she were a sacrament by which she wished to communicate his life to me." The author expressed this in a prayer that we recited in the seminaries on the eve of Vatican II: "O Jesus living in Mary…"

MICHEL DE SAINT-AUGUSTIN († 1684)

He was a Flemish Carmelite of the old order (from the Tours reform), born Michel Van Ballart in 1621; he taught theology and was three times the provincial of the Belgian province. His writings reflect a whole treatise on the life of union with Mary, based on a mystical experience he encountered. According to the doctrine of the fathers of the Church, God decided not to grant any grace to human-kind unless it passes through the hands of Mary, and this is why they call her the "neck" of the Church (Saint Bernard).

These texts underwent many reprints and partial translations between the years 1928 and 1957 (under quite different titles) during the most recent days of the Marian movement, and there were also partial translations of the two books by Michel de Saint Augustin.[30] The title of *The Mariform Life* seemed to introduce a construction that gave Mary a similar function to that ascribed to the Holy

Spirit when we say it is "the (transcendent) soul of the Church" (*transcendent* is used here to make it clear that we are not speaking of an incarnation of the Holy Spirit, but rather that he respects and raises up people who form the Church). Right from the first page, Michel de Saint Augustin explains this somewhat disturbing concept in quite an unassuming way:

> *Deiformiter, id est conformiter Dei beneplacito,*
> *Mariaeformiter: seu conformiter beneplacito Dei genitricis*
> *Mariae.*
> Deiform, in a Godlike way, that is in conformity with
> God's good pleasure.
> Mariform, that is in conformity with the good pleasure of
> Mary, the Mother of God.

The expression therefore means only compliance with the pleasure of Mary, as an imitation, without ontological or metaphysical pretensions.

Several times he refers to the Carmelite Peter Thomas and believes that "no grace is given to men without passing through the hands of Mary." He invites them to live, to act, and to die "in Mary and for Mary," as its title indicates. But he remains theocentric—he began his treatise with the Deiform life and he considers the Mariform life as a form of this divine life. His title, which places the Deiform life first, ends with a clause stating that we must worship God in spirit and in truth. So there is no ambiguity on that point. He invites us to reach a state where the spirit of Mary directs, owns, galvanizes, and enlivens the soul, so that it is somehow transformed into Mary: "*Quasi Transformatus.*"

MARY OF SAINT THERESE (DIED 1677)

Although he does not name her in his Treatise (through discretion), Michel de Saint Augustin seems to be the interpreter of the mystical experience of Mary Petyt, his directee (Mary of Saint Therese in religion), a Carmelite tertiary. At 34, she had made the acquaintance of the young Carmelite (aged 36), in Ghent. She had followed him to Mechelen where, in 1659, he wrote his *Treatise on the Deiform and Mariform Life*. Six years after the death of Mary of Saint Therese, he published her life story,[31] interspersed with spiritual sayings. How did he learn this doctrine? Was she his source? Only a systematic long-term study could establish that. Since he was the editor of all that came to light, Michel de Saint Augustin could have made his mark upon it, but that is not evident from a stylistic point of view. We might ask, for example, if the following expression of Marie of Saint Therese, at the beginning of the doctrinal chapter,[32] may not have come from the director rather than the directee:

> God's grace has allowed me to experience this life in Mary, for her, with and through her…so that one who lives only in pure divinity, can practice it with a similar simplicity, etc.[33]

His writing tends toward the theological and the abstract. Marie of Saint Therese's texts, apart from the one already quoted, are presented in a regular way, in expressions that are spontaneous, original, tentative, like an experience without any logical order. She does not speak of the Mariform life and refrains from any theory or systematic phrase, but reflects what she feels, with images that sometimes accumulate in an attempt to say the unsayable.

His relationship with his directee makes us think of that of Hans Urs von Balthasar with Adrienne von Speyr, but on the level of mystical experience rather than theological intuition. We can reconstruct how it played out as follows:[34] from childhood, Mary Petyt, a little girl from the bourgeoisie of Ghent, feels a strong call, but it does not prevent her thinking of marriage. She was lacing up her corset with considerable energy trying to make her waist as thin as possible, as part of her strenuous efforts to look "pretty" (p. 8), when the divine call led her first into the canonesses regular of Saint Augustine, in Ghent. However, an eye disease forced her to leave the Order, and she became aware of a call to the solitary life of a hermit. She lived alone in the small béguinage of Ghent, and this is where she met the Carmelites of the Ancient Observance, who understood her desire to meet God alone in the desert. One of them already discerned that she was "called to such a solitary life that no convent would be able to give her." She then made the acquaintance of Michel de Saint Augustin, who understood her thoroughly. She followed him to Malines in 1657, and then lived in the convent of the Hermitage until her death in 1677. She was tertiary Carmelite and not formally a recluse (p. 7). According to Louis Van den Bossche, her orientation is characterized by the following features:

> She made extreme (and perhaps excessive) distinctions between the various powers of the soul: the operation of intelligence and the will, according to the model described by Tauler and Albert the Great. In other words, she isolated the depths of the soul (the *mens* and the natural will) not only from the material and sensible world but especially from reason and will, by exercising discipline at all times over the minutest of actions. This was her intimate, compelling and consistent vocation: a vocation of the desert, which responded well to the spirit of Carmel.[35]

This passivity caused her to say toward the end of her life: "Anyone else would have done the same in my place."

Such passivity must be understood in the sense of high receptivity. Her problem was finding a way of articulating the natural and supernatural. She achieved this less by "subordination" than by "separation, isolation, flight" (p. 10), like a hermit: "A retreat into the depths of one's soul as though in a desert," where God acts. She is very conscious of this.

Her relationship to Mary is rooted in communal devotion and in that of the Carmelites, whom the people called "brothers of the Virgin," a title they favored very much. But the intimate place she retired to, at least in the year 1668, was an innovation in the Carmelite tradition. Two factors guided her growth: (1) She avoided any special devotion, treating it as a screen between God and the spirit; (2) Her inner stirrings profoundly transformed her devotion.

Almost all texts date her experience of Mary from 1668 (one is from 1659, one from 1666, three from 1669, and one from 1670). The year 1668, however, marks a decisive moment: her spiritual marriage with God and the privileged place that Mary takes. It is believed to have occurred three times. In the first stage, the Virgin appears to her, on February 4, 1659.[36] This visit is deeply marked by infused and passive grace and prompts her to consecrate everything to Mary, especially the girls who have been entrusted to her. In the second stage, at Candlemas, 1666, Mary appears to her carrying the child Jesus, and she puts him in her arms.

Unlike the previous apparition, it seemed to me that there was some analogy with the description given by Saint Teresa of some revelation she had from the kind Mother and kind Father (Joseph). She paid no special attention to any particular point about their persons, but, to the satisfaction of her soul, she took in at a glance the whole person of the kind Mother (p. 38).

The two (Mary and Joseph) were one, and the one was made up of two. In addition, this aspect was contained in the oneness of the Divine Being (p. 38). The fact that all this is given by God, who is never lost sight of, is a constant factor of his relationships.

In the third stage, in 1668 (the date is not specified in the texts at our disposal), a new event occurs, this time no longer just apparitions, but the very experience of her living presence:

> It seems to me that these kinds of representations and the motions I experienced are now withdrawing from me. Things, now, become more and more abstract. It is not that their being withdraws, but, it seems to me, I taste them in a way that is more exalted and stranger to my senses. There is no doubt that they brought to an end the place to which the previous experiences were headed. In fact...their sweet inspirations seem to have...disposed me...to a closer and more prominent loving union with my divine friend (Christ) where my heart was more deeply wounded by his divine love. They made me more intimate with him. (pp. 38–39)

Other texts make clear that Mary disappears in order to give place to Christ at the time of the mystical marriage, in order to leave her alone with the Bridegroom (Christ):

> One day, as I presented our food to the kind Mother for her to bless...as she taught me to do, it came suddenly to my mind the thought that the kind Mother was not coming as often as before. I was surprised not to enjoy her frequent presence nor her instructions or affectionate words. And yet my love for her was so tender, innocent, filial and sweet as ever. Then this inner response was born in me:

When the kind Mother was always beside you and she guided you in the ways of virtue, it was to prepare you for the spiritual marriage with her beloved [son, to allow you] to converse alone with the Bridegroom, as appropriate.

Indeed, since the union took place [the spiritual marriage to Christ], my soul has usually been alone with the Beloved. The kind Mother and the angels appear to remain outside.

In short, we go from an ordinary devotion that deepens into apparitions, to an infused presence that is strongly felt, then an eclipse of Mary's presence to give place to Christ alone, while God alone from the outset penetrates and animates everything. Mary remains present, without being perceived or felt.

This progression is a sign of authenticity. There are others too. Marie of Saint Therese is direct and without any complacency. She takes this presence to be an undeserved grace that inspires humility (pp. 33, 72). She kept the secret of these graces until her death (p. 86). These experiences carry for her certain fruits, including a grace of evangelical childhood: "For as long as the presence of the kind Mother lasts, I see in me an exceptional childlike candor" (etc., p. 32).

She uses images of all kinds: fusion (p. 77), light (pp. 77, 96), human expressions of affection such as cuddling and caressing (pp. 75–76), the fire and flame of love (p. 93), and anointing (p. 87). This diversity of language serves to convey an ineffable experience and these images seem quite coherent. If she developed (p. 53) the image of Marian mediation, "Everything must pass through the hands of Mary as rain passes through the gutter" (p. 53), this formulation (that of her director) hardly appears anywhere else but here. She usually relates her experience in a more spontaneous way.

This introspective analysis, centered on the search for God alone, might appear to err due to its lack of focus on others. We would have liked to know more about the fruits of charity. But in fact they are not absent. She expresses this two or three times, in the seventy-five pages available to us.

> Another consequence of [this grace] is to increase my zeal and eagerness to spread the worship and glory of her. I would like to draw everyone to love her, serve her, devote themselves to her, and in all their spiritual and temporal needs, to gently and lovingly have recourse to her with confidence, [I feel led to] entrust to her...all the needs...of others.
>
> If this fervor were to persist a little...my nature would be turned upside down....I would be so good, so tender, so welcoming, so kind, so gentle, so humble, so nice, generous and charitable to everyone without exception. And if my poverty prevents me from actually realizing that generosity and charity towards all who are in need, I must, nevertheless, carry these virtues ingrained deeply within me, and my heart is filled with love and compassion and the desire to help everyone....Though our nature be already transformed in these aspects, I would it were even more, so that I could assimilate the nature and spirit of our kind Mother like a true child. (p. 69)
>
> I think I suckled on the kind mother's compassionate spirit while she was with me so long, teaching me her mind and nature as though I were a child. Because, from that moment on, those feelings of devotion and sweet sympathy have remained in me without interruption. Before that time, I was quite impassive by nature. I had no

inclination to loving dedication, and any tendency towards kindness, or benevolence towards my neighbor was quite foreign to me. Now I feel completely filled internally as with the oil of benevolence, kindness, and love towards all. Blessed be the Immaculate Virgin and Mother who has transformed me, and seems to have given birth to me again in God. She has infused me with another nature, another spirit, which are more consistent with her nature and her spirit.[37]

Finally, Mary of Saint Therese made quite clear the distinction between the transcendent presence of God and Mary's presence (p. 50):

In tasting of God, I also tasted of Mary, as though she were one with God and not distinct from him. God and Mary seem to be for the soul one object, almost in the manner of the sacred humanity of Christ, as we, while united with the divinity, contemplate and perceive these two natures as one person and one object [of contemplation].

Although there is in Mary no personal union with the deity, as is the case with Christ, but only a holy and free union, it is still infinitely more excellent in her than in the most eminent of creatures. To those whose soul contemplates, God shows Mary perfectly united with Him and united to Him without enabling us to distinguish any intermediary level in this union.

This is a similar intuition to that of Father Maximilian Kolbe, who considered Mary to show God transparently (and especially of the Holy Spirit, but he also distinguished less clearly the difference between this transparency of union and the hypostatic union).

Another sign of authenticity is that Mary of Saint Therese traced her progress against superficial Marian experiences where Mary would appear to screen the soul from God. To those who see Mary as "an impediment to pure union and fruition in God," she replied (p. 61):

> There is not, in this case, the slightest impediment or means interposed between the supreme Good, the pure being of God, and the soul. Rather, there is help provided for the soul, to allow it to reach God more easily and to be more fully established in Him....Filial love for Mary does not bring harm to divine life in God....The Spirit of God acts in due course, without the bond and union with God becoming more mediated, but in such a way that they find nourishment and a firmer foundation for their godly and divine life.

Here she is referring to a particular grace and experience. Care must be taken because the intense Marian presence she felt is specific to the time (mainly texts of 1668). Afterward, Mary seems to disappear and instead leads to Christ alone, in the sense of the Gospel story about the marriage feast at Cana: "Do whatever he tells you."

Michel de Saint Augustine expresses his experiences of a theology that was favored during the Spanish Golden Age. It can be particularly surprising when he says that contemplating Mary and God together is "more perfect than the contemplation of God alone" because it adds an accidental perfection. Nevertheless, the intention with this particular formulation is to fully uphold theocentrism.

JOHN EUDES (DIED 1680)

He was the subject of a monograph by Charles Chesnay.[38] None of his formal texts use the word *presence*, but a corresponding underlying experience seems to be in effect and was perceived by those who knew him; Mary "was always present in his mind," wrote Pierre Costile.[39] "She guided him in all his actions."[40]

A more explicit text can be found in the *Constitutions of the Sisters of Our Lady of Charity*, drafted by Saint John Eudes (p. 168):

> Live the life of the Sacred Heart. Have His senti-ments ever in your hearts, dispose yourselves according to his will, follow his inclinations, love what he loves..., give yourself constantly to his Spirit, so that the same spirit may *possess you and lead you in all things*, that his grace may sanctify you, that his charity may enflame you, his love set you ablaze, his zeal for the salvation of souls consume you.[41]

These terms suggest more than an imitation or influence of the spirit of the Heart of Mary, so it appears to be from Mary herself.

MARY OF THE INCARNATION (DIED 1672)

Born Marie Guyart in 1599, she was married for a year to Claude Martin (who died very soon afterward). She had gained a deep mystical life, involving a radical religious vocation that her spiritual director and her family had mis-understood in marrying her off at age 19, according to the custom of the time. Her providential widowhood opened her eyes to her vocation. She raised her son for twelve years, and then left him with her family to go to Quebec. Her mission was given to her by a vision of the Virgin, which was an exceptional grace, but is beside the point, for the moment. But she is also cited as one of the witnesses who experienced the habitual presence of the Virgin. In fact, she only used the word *presence* once to describe a momentary grace in 1651, which she bore witness to in 1654.

She then directed that a building be constructed that she had dedicated to Our Lady and held as the property of the Blessed Virgin, "the first and perpetual Superior" of the house. She writes:

[on the Vision relating to her vocation of May 3, 1635]:

The Blessed Virgin sat holding the baby Jesus in her arms. I eagerly ran towards her extending my arms, holding them out to the ends of the seat where she sat....The Blessed Virgin glanced at this place so distressed, while I burned with the desire to see the face of the Mother of Beautiful Fondness, for I could only see her back. As I was engaged in these thoughts, she turned her head toward me and, showing me her face with a beautiful smile, gave me a kiss. She turned also to her child, Jesus, speaking to him in secret as though about me. She did the same three times. My companion, who had already taken a step on the path leading down had no share in the caresses of the Blessed Virgin, she had only the consolation of hearing the voice from the place where she was.... The pleasure I felt from such a pleasant thing can not be explained. Thereupon, I awoke still enjoying the sweetness that I had experienced, which lasted several days...

I felt a great inner attraction from it, along with an instruction to make a house for Jesus and Mary.[42]

In 1651:

Having thus understood his will and that he wanted to use me to manage our recovery, any aversion that I had towards this plan passed from my mind. I felt strong and of good courage (note: the work began on May 19th) knowing that I belonged to the Blessed Virgin and our most worthy Mother and Superior. I call her "Our Superior" because some time before the fire took place, Reverend Mother St. Athanasius, our Superior, had a strong inspiration to give it back and place control into her hands, begging her to be our first and principle superior. We did this with great solemnity, rendering her our homage and recognition of her as our first and perpetual superior. So I regarded this plan, as my highest priority after God. I had no sooner begun work than I felt her assistance in a very extraordinary way, in that I felt her to be present with me at all times. I did not see her with bodily eyes nor in an imaginary vision, but the way the most adorable incarnate Word did me the honor and mercy of communicating himself to me, through union with him, through love and current and constant communication, that I have never experienced with regard to the Blessed Virgin, Mother of God, was such that on this occasion, although I would have him always with me, I had an even greater devotion. But here also the union that I had with her in my heart, allowed me to speak to her through loving activity that was very simple and intense in the depth of my soul, as though to her beloved Son; I felt her there without seeing her near me, accompanying me throughout the comings and goings that were required for the building work, since we had begun to break down hovels with the aim of finishing the work. Along the way, I would talk to her, saying: "Come, Divine Mother, let us go to see our workers." As required by the work, I would go upstairs, downstairs, on scaffolding, without any fear....Sometimes, I felt inspired to honor her by some of the Church's hymns or anthems. I followed all her movements and often said to her: "My divine Mother, please watch over our workers. And it is true that she looked after them so well that during the building work and construction, not one of them was injured. Because of my weakness I needed these helps in all the tiredness I had to bear and the arrangements I had to make....Nevertheless, I experienced what Our Lord said of his burden, that it is easy and light, that I felt myself to be in the company of his most holy Mother. From that time on, I knew by the communication I had with a person who has received great graces from God, that some time after our fire, the Holy Virgin in an intellectual vision, revealed to her and assured her that it was she who would repair the ruins of our house and that she would look after it. She even told her other secrets, which were not about me, which I will speak about in good time,...because this good soul has fully informed me what the Divine Majesty told her, for which she said to her: "Do you not believe it, my daughter?" She told her yes. Three times she asked the same thing, and for evidence that she believed the divine Mother, she signed it with her blood. I only found out about it about two years later, and she does not know what happened to me in loving communication with which it has pleased the Divine Mother of goodness to honor me.[43]

This was an intense period of Mary's presence. It was an invisible presence that required faith, but it was also exceptional, extraordinary, and probably temporary and momentary (like that of Therese of Lisieux, who lived for three days as though hidden beneath the mantle of the Virgin, in the second state). It is an inner union that combines contemplation and efficacy, with fruits of peace and freedom. Her son, Dom Claude Martin (whom she had entrusted to the Virgin Mary on leaving) emphasizes this grace: "But there was no danger for her: The Holy Virgin accompanied her everywhere, not only in an intellectual manner, but also by the presence she experienced and could almost touch."[44]

MARGARET-MARY ALACOQUE (DIED 1690)

Margaret-Mary Alacoque insists on filial belonging:[45]

"She became so much mistress of my heart, that I became like one of her own; she ruled me."

Since I was only young I did not dare to address myself to her Son, but always to her....Like a little child, I spoke to her very simply.[46]

One day she received this response to her cries of anguish:[47]

You will be my true daughter and I will be your good Mother.

And she heard the Lord say to her:[48]

I put you under the care of my Mother that she may mold you according to my plans.

Again she writes:[49]

The Blessed Virgin rewarded me with her presence, embraced me warmly and told me: "My dear daughter, you still have a long road to travel."

ARNAULD (MARIE-CLAIRE)

This apparition occurred at Port Royal, to Sister Marie-Claire Arnauld, who calls Mary: "The only way in which I can expect God's mercy." She also adds: "Most of my time is taken up with her and I cannot live except under her shadow."[50]

LOUIS-MARIE GRIGNION DE MONTFORT (DIED 1716)

He returns several times to this theme in *The Secret of Mary*:

> *In Jacob inhabita: in electis meis mitte radices*: My faithful wife, put down roots among my chosen ones. Whoever is chosen and predestined for Mary, staying close to her, that is to say in their hearts, he allows to take root in deep humility and ardent charity, and in all the virtues.[51]

And more formally:

> Take much care not to torment yourself, if you do not enjoy early the sweet presence of the Holy Virgin within you. This grace is not given to everyone, and when God favors a soul in his great mercy, it is easy to lose if one is not faithful in recollecting oneself often; and if this misfortune does happen to you, come back and sweetly make amends to your sovereign.[52]
>
> The experience will teach you infinitely more than I can tell you.[53]

This is the same experience that is referred to in nos. 47, 54, 55, and 57 of *The Secret of Mary*:

No. 47: We must always act in Mary, that is to say, we must gradually acquire the habit of recollecting ourselves interiorly and so form within us an idea or a spiritual image of Mary. She must become, as it were, an Oratory for the soul where we offer up our prayers to God without fear of being ignored. She will be as a Tower of David for us where we can seek safety from all our enemies. She will be a burning lamp lighting up our inmost soul and inflaming us with love for God. She will be a sacred place of repose where we can contemplate God in her company. Finally Mary will be the only means we will use in going to God, and she will become our intercessor for everything we need. When we pray we will pray in Mary. When we receive Jesus in Holy Communion we will place him in Mary for him to take his delight in her. If we do anything at all, it will be in Mary, and in this way Mary will help us to forget self everywhere and in all things.

No. 54: Let us set to work, then, dear soul, through perseverance in the living of this devotion, in order that Mary's soul may glorify the Lord in us and her spirit be within us to rejoice in God her Saviour (Lk 1:46). These are the words of St. Ambrose.[54]

No. 55: This devotion faithfully practiced produces countless happy effects in the soul. The most important of them is that it establishes, even here on earth, Mary's life in the soul, so that it is no longer the soul that lives, but Mary who lives in it. In a manner of speaking, Mary's soul becomes identified with the soul of her servant. Indeed when by an unspeakable but real grace Mary most holy becomes Queen of a soul, she works untold wonders in it. She is a great wonder-worker especially in the interior of souls. She works there in secret, unsuspected by the soul, as knowledge of it might destroy the beauty of her work.

No. 57: To sum up, Mary becomes all things for the soul that wishes to serve Jesus Christ. She enlightens its mind with her pure faith. She deepens its heart with her humility. She enlarges and inflames its heart with her charity, makes it pure with her purity, makes it noble and great through her motherly care. But why dwell any longer on this? Experience alone will teach us the wonders wrought by Mary in the soul, wonders so great that the wise and the proud, and even a great number of devout people find it hard to credit them.

This theme is developed more formally in the *Treatise on True Devotion*:

No. 46: At the end of the world…, the greatest saints…will be the most faithful in prayer to the Most Holy Virgin and keeping her always present, as their perfect model to imitate her and as their powerful help.

No. 152: [Through true devotion] Mary makes herself so near and present to her faithful servants, to enlighten them…to strengthen them…that truly the virginal way to find Jesus Christ is a path of roses and honey. He invites us to "remain in Mary" and see there the source of great spiritual benefits. (no. 263–65)

The theme returns in canticle 77, verses 6 and 15:

She is my divine oratory
Where I always find Jesus

There I pray with glory...
Here is what we can only believe:
I carry her within me,
Engraved with lines of glory,
Although in the darkness of faith.

He invites us to "remain in Mary" and see there the source of great spiritual benefits (no. 263–65). This experience is attested by other authors of the eighteenth century, for example by J. P. Boffarel:

The Church experiences the love of our Mother and the abundance of her sweetness....Under the protection of such a Mother, the hearts of the children of God rejoice. And we have no doubt she bears towards us (*eam affici erga nos*) the affection that mothers usually have towards their children.[55]

J. E. Rottner[56] develops the following themes: Mary's presence is everywhere. The virtue (power) of Mary's presence (No. 1003–21, p. 436–45) appears in the commentary on John 2:1, *Paraenensis* 46.

D. Gleich develops the theme that the final index summarizes as follows: "Her memory and her presence are very sweet to both angels and human beings."[57]

PETER-JOSEPH DE CLORIVIÈRE (DIED 1820)

At the turn of the eighteenth and nineteenth centuries, the priest of Clorivière returns several times to this experience, which he sees as a requirement:

Towards the end of my prayer, it seemed to me that those words were said to me inwardly, as from Our Lady: Go your way under my protection. If I accompany you, you will reach the end. At that moment I was filled with the sweet feeling of her presence. I begged, since it had pleased her to receive me as a son, that she make me well worthy of the name, protesting that I wanted nothing more than to become a vivid image of her and her Son, suffering, despised and crucified.[58]

Retreat of 1769:

After supper, having said the Rosary and being more recollected than usual, it seemed to me that Our Lady was present although she was invisible: this caused me to address my prayers to her with unusual fervor....It seemed to me that Our Lady adopted me as one of her children and gave me her blessing.[59]

And in a text from 1771:

What state would I die in? Saved from hell through the merits of Jesus Christ, preserved from Purgatory by the intercession and very special protection of Mary.

The presence of Jesus and Mary, the sweet conversations I had with them in my mind, in my heart, in the center of my soul, it is that that I now hope to find.[60]

This is a symbol: Mary, the "Tower of David" and "sacred altar," a spiritual theology, but also a testimony and an invitation to a profound experience.

On the life of Louis Marie Grignion de Montfort, the priest of Clorivière reports what was said by Blin, a friend of de Montfort:

The "name of Mary" was constantly on his lips....He took care to make continual homage to her and the memory of the Mother of God was so imprinted on his mind and in his heart that he would never lose sight of it, so that, as he himself said to someone, he was constantly in her presence and under her eyes.[61]

WILLIAM-JOSEPH CHAMINADE (DIED 1824)

In a sense, Chaminade came up with his own theory of Mary's presence: "There are some who have the gift of the presence of Jesus Christ and the Virgin Mary, but this is very rare. One has to be very faithful to deserve it."[62] He had composed a consecration to God through Mary that is read every day in the congregation he founded—the Marianists, which is a word he made up in order not to clash with the tradition of the Marists.

In the book entitled *Life in Union with Mary*, Neubert (died 1967) has the same thought although in a more precise form, as found in *The Spirit of our Foundation*, Society of Mary (t. 1, p. 173): "The gift of the habitual presence of the Blessed Virgin, just like the gift of the habitual presence of God, is very rare, it is true, but is accessible to those who exhibit great faithfulness."[63]

In the context of the two editions already cited, Chaminade specifies that the Blessed Virgin is not among us in the same way that Our Lord Jesus Christ is, but she looks upon us from heaven where she reigns.[64] In other words, this presence is at the same time linked to that of Christ, dependent but different (less extreme). It is from this perspective that he invites us to cultivate this experience:

In the presence of God, the children of Mary join the presence of their mother! From heaven, her eyes are fixed on her children. She is always willing to help them in their prayers and in their battles. Let us never lose sight of that sweet thought; she is also faithful and consoling.

Once you have experienced these different ways in which God is present, you also place yourself in the presence of the Blessed Virgin. You will see her in heaven beside her divine Son, eyes turned towards you: you shall offer him your services as your sovereign, you ask her to assist you as your good mother....You will end, as the method suggests, by commending yourself to Him and offering yourself to God and the Blessed Virgin with the resolutions you have taken.[65]

The following text provides a biblical background, in reference to John 19:25–27:

Here is your Mother: Our Lord was dying and it seemed that the Blessed Virgin had no Son. Our Lord gives her to the disciple St. John to take the place of Jesus Christ; Our Lord therefore means that Mary should become his Mother, it means that she carries the love and tenderness she had for Jesus Christ....Have we heard deep within our hearts these words that Jesus Christ also speaks to us from the Cross: *Ecce Mater tua*? What does our heart say because of the most venerable Mary....Rejoice...That all the world may know that we are true children of Mary, especially by our purity.[66]

JEAN-MARIE VIANNEY (DIED 1859)

This grace is attributed to the Curé d'Ars by the apostolic process: "All were convinced that he enjoyed the presence of the Holy Virgin in a special way."[67]

LOUIS-EDWARD CESTAC (DIED 1868)

He describes his experience less like contemplation and more like action: "No, I do not see her, but I sense her presence, like a horse senses the hand of the rider who guides it."[68]

ESTELLE FAGUETTE (DIED 1876)

The visionary of Pellevoisin, who was abandoned by the doctors, was miraculously healed after hearing these words: "Fear nothing, you know well that you are my child...I will be invisibly close to you."[69]

THÉRÈSE OF THE CHILD JESUS (DIED 1897)

"Little Thérèse" had this experience in 1889 that she reported on her deathbed, July 11, 1897:

> For me it was like a veil thrown over everything on the earth...I was entirely hidden under the veil of the Holy Virgin. During that time, I was in charge of the refectory and I remember I was doing things as if I were not doing them; it was as if someone had lent me a body. I remained in that state for a whole week.[70]

MARIE-COLETTE DU SACRÉ COEUR (DIED 1905) FROM BESANÇON

> I find myself very often praying that the Blessed Virgin will deign to prepare me to receive Our Lord in Holy Communion. I am so unworthy of so great a work, and all my preparations are so little, that I am comforted that my dear Heavenly Mother wants to come to my rescue, giving me her heart sometimes and also the dispositions that she herself had. And this love I felt for our Lord in the

Blessed Sacrament, and which seemed so lacking in fervor previously is nothing more than coldness and indifference in comparison to what I now feel for Him. It seems to me that this is nothing but a small flame escaping from a narrow and poor heart, but what consumes me is a very huge fiery furnace of love for the adorable Sacrament, which is my God himself, full of love for me which he gives me every day.[71]

And elsewhere: "It seems to me now that she never leaves me. Even though she is not visible to me, I feel her presence and her protection."[72]

CHRISTINE LUCIE (DIED 1908)

Quoted by Auguste Poulain:

Sometimes the soul is particularly united to the Blessed Virgin, so that it feels like a blessed link tightening its union with Our Lord. (p. 65)
This union has this peculiarity that the soul feels the Blessed Virgin as a bond of love between God and itself, like a divine intermediary. (p. 29)
The Blessed Mother is the link, the intermediary, whether we feel it or not, between God and us. Jesus has allowed me to see and feel it more than I can express, at least for now. (p. 139)[73]

MARIE-ANTOINETTE DE GEUSER (NICKNAMED "CONSUMMATA," DIED 1920)

It is as if God…has transformed me into Mary (I do not understand how this could be done, but the only word I can use to describe what has happened is "transform"). I felt as though I was participating in Mary's reign as Queen of Martyrs….It seems to me she asked me to call myself Mary of the Trinity. But that's merely a detail.

ANGELA SORAZU (DIED 1921)

Angela Sorazu was a Conceptionist Franciscan and reported the following experience:

> About August 1894 my anxieties increased that I possess the Virgin Mary as my heritage....One day, when I was more inflamed with love for Mary, and more anxious to possess her, I felt favored with her presence and saw how she possessed my soul and my body whose members and feelings, which were devoted to her service, were sanctified and belonged to her. At the same time I began to feel clearly the presence of the Madonna in the depths of my being....I felt very happy as though I had everything. Therefore, in a few days [it was] as if the Madonna had enlarged my soul to make room for God. I felt inflamed with divine ardor, and I was anxious to have God as my own.[74]
>
> Frequently then I enjoyed the presence of the Virgin in a transitory way, as if, so to speak, she was in the bosom of God when I adored the divinity, or when I sensed the presence of God in me as vivid reality. Other times I enjoyed the presence of God in the Madonna as if she contained God within her. In this case, I saw the Madonna as an immense light extending out to all creation like a spiritual world or heaven on earth.[75]

MARIE BONAVENTURE FINK (DIED 1922)

A little before her death, this servant of God, a sister in the Schools of Notre-Dame, expressed her previous experiences like this: "Now everything is silent. The old nature is dead. For this reason, my Mother is present more freely, in a more pure way and it is as if she were enthroned in me with her spirit."[76]

DOM EDOUARD POPPE (DIED 1924)

This servant of God described well the boundaries of his experience:

> I unite myself to Mary in order to talk, and to listen to her speak to me; in prayer I unite myself to her and let her guide me; if I have doubts as to the solution to some problem, I appeal to her for help: I contemplate Jesus in the Blessed Sacrament with the eyes and heart of Mary. This union and operation of Mary in me gives me no sense of consolation, but increases my confidence and strength....Again I add: Mary gives way to Jesus, or rather manifests herself in her relationship with him. So, I see Jesus when I contemplate Mary, and it is Jesus who dominates [*primeggia*] alone in this devotion, no matter how specifically Marian it is. I never see Mary separated from Jesus; but she introduced me to him...through her maternal relationship with Jesus, and through contemplating the life, work and divinity of her Son....She does not reveal him, but she is herself an almost necessary revelation of Him.[77]

SILVIO GALOTTI (DIED 1927)

Servant of God, Oblate of Saints Gaudens and Charles, says quite plainly:[78] "I see the Madonna at all times so near, that I feel no longer able to live but in her. I feel that the little good that I do is neither the work nor the fruit of my industry. The Madonna who is in me is the one who works."[79]

MARIA DI SANTA CECILIA (DIED 1929)

She was from the Congregation of Jesus and Mary, and she has similar comments in her autobiography: "The good Master has taken away my heart and has put in its place his own Sacred Heart and the Immaculate Heart of Mary. It is a divine operation that the pen cannot describe. I can no longer search outside of Jesus and Mary, but I possess them intimately."[80]

FATHER VAYSSIÈRE, OP (DIED 1940)

He was a provincial from Toulouse and led an austere life, completely oriented toward Mary: "The Holy Virgin is our mother, she loves us like a mother, we should love her like our mother."[81]

He lost his mother at a very young age. Again he says:[82]

The more one attends to Mary and her works, the more one is on the way to union with God, to reliving the life of Jesus....We must establish ourselves spiritually in Mary like a child in the womb of his mother. The more we are united to her, the more she enlivens us. It is she, it is Mary who forms us....The way of filial loyalty to Mary is the true way; believe this. It is like reliving the very life of Jesus of Nazareth.

The more we are little, the more we can allow her to be Mother. The child means more to his mother when it is weaker and smaller....Perfection of the way of childhood in the divine plan, is the life of Mary.[83]

He explains: "The Blessed Virgin is an essential agent of the spiritual life, especially at the more advanced levels."[84] He gives her this exalted position without dissociating himself from her and without her getting in the way. On the contrary:[85]

> Mary is like a great river carrying us to Christ (he says). But we must believe that Mary and Our Lord are only stages in taking us to the Father. No, that's not right. Mary, Christ, and God are one; they are inseparable!
>
> All Mary's actions lead to Jesus....We cannot conceive in her any part of her activity that would not have Jesus as its object and purpose. It is her mission. She is the mother. Her role as mother is to give us divine life in exchange for all that she gives us to sacrifice....It is the Holy Spirit himself who created and prepared Mary's heart, and who has plumbed his ineffable depths. He has given her the heart of a mother...like God's heart..., and it is with this heart that is made for God, with her tenderness reserved for God, that Mary loves humanity, loves each one of our souls.[86]

H. Lefranc makes another comment in *Sint Unum*: "I would like to end this retreat with a consecration to the Sacred Heart, and I feel an irresistible urge to consecrate myself to Mary."[87] In a letter to a directee from the solitude of Saint Baume, he explains Mary's presence like this:

> I trust that you understand more and more that She is the true way to Jesus....The perfection of the way of childhood in God's plan is the life of Mary....So, always remain in this sweet atmosphere of Mary. Wherever you are...never act

alone, but focus on Mary in all things, not only on her thoughts, but on her presence, in filial trust....But above all, in those hours of doubt and testing, turn to Mary: she is never more present and active than at that moment.

ANSELM TREVES, OMI, SERVANT OF GOD (DIED 1934)

I strive to make room in myself not for a virtual but for a real conversation with the Madonna.[88]

I wish that in my life I will continue to look towards her. I can habitually think of her.[89] It seems to me that the Madonna has given me the grace to be able to think of her more easily; and I usually strive not to lose sight of my Mother even for a moment. That is easy to do when I am grading papers; and also when I am in class I usually have her before my eyes.[90]

JOSEPH SHELLHORN (DIED 1935)

Servant of God, Marianist novice master, he asked for this gift in prayer. He makes reference to it when he writes: "From the ever-growing union with Mary, we will derive all good. When Mary is present, spiritual work and apostolic activity reach their maximum.[91] My usual disposition seems to be that I live and act directly dependent on Mary with filial union and trust."[92]

MARIE-REINE DE JESUS (DIED 1938)

Servant of God, daughter of Mary Immaculate, who offered herself as a victim for France in 1936. She said, a little afterward: "I hardly leave my mother. It is she who does everything. She has pity on her child."[93] But it is

Jesus she thanks for the peace she found in renewing her offering.

MUTIEN-MARIE DE CINEY (DIED MAY 15, 1940)

He was a Belgian religious, a Brother of the Christian Schools, who was the victim of a train wreck. From his childhood, he had the desire to "love the Blessed Virgin as she has never been loved before." On January 30, 1917, his uncle, who was also a Brother of the Christian Schools, died. He had asked Mary that she might accompany his nephew everywhere and she gave him "that grace." When his uncle died, at 4:30 a.m., Brother Mutien felt such love for the Virgin that he cried out, "Lord, who is this great saint to whom I owe this increase in love?" Later he stated, "My mother came; she is so good; she made me taste her presence, and I found myself given up to a state that lasted for three weeks."

He writes to one of his brothers in religion, on April 19, 1917: "Suffering is a grace of choice; it is a kiss from Jesus. Do you remember that night when Jesus came to visit us with Mary, when this good Mother made you feel his presence? Jesus then asked if you wanted to suffer a little for him. And you answered: 'Anything you want, Jesus!'"

LEONARD (DIED 1946)

Servant of God (SC) he wrote:

> To live in the presence of Mary and seek to please her in order to please God....The general intention of pleasing Mary causes a double movement in my soul: one of recollection, the other of yearning..., recollection in order to place myself in contact with Mary and convince me of her presence.[94]

XANTHIN LEONARD (DIED 1946)

He was a Brother of the Christian Schools who was blessed with a transparent love for Our Lady, and left some spiritual notebooks where we read:

> At every moment, to die to myself, to destroy something of myself, so that I can live in Mary, with Mary.
>
> To stop living for myself in order to live for Mary; she herself is identified with Jesus....My good and tender Mother, I am not worthy, but if you are so merciful, grant me the gift of your presence as you promised with great faithfulness.[95]
>
> Grant that I may believe in your presence in seeing, in acting and in loving; that I may have more of the joy of your presence.
>
> But, my mother, you are here. Vision, action and mystical union: a threefold way of being present and a source of ineffable consolation.

Father Lefranc[96] found in this remark the principle of its synthesis: vision, action, and mystical union, as we shall see later.

REGINALD GARRIGOU-LAGRANGE (DIED 1964)

He was a Dominican theologian and was an authority on the structures and concepts of the theology of Thomas Aquinas. His life and spiritual experience were profound, and he was in contact with many mystics and directees to whom he was a knowledgeable guide. What he has to say about his experience is worthwhile. He recognized that the experience of the presence of Mary was a genuine phenomenon of spiritual life. His theological explanation of its cause flawlessly fits the facts, but nowadays we look for closer ties between abstract analysis and the spiritual phenomena as manifested in psychological life. As a classical theologian, he could interpret the spiritual life that he was experiencing and knew well the nature of its instrumental causality, whose mechanisms he analyzed as much as possible.

PIERRE-MARIE THÉAS (BISHOP OF LOURDES, DIED APRIL 3, 1977)

He too experienced this grace in faith. He invited the faithful to live like him and to follow his example.

WORKS AND REFLECTION

After the war of 1940, this type of mystical literature, where moods and experiences were exposed, gives way to a realistic and missionary perspective. I have not found any significant texts after this date. There only remains for us to consider studies on the presence of Mary. These occur between the years 1937 and 1960: a collection of texts from Neubert and H. Lefranc, which we have collated and completed, and a spiritual or doctrinal assessment (the same as R. Garrigou-Lagrange).

EMIL NEUBERT, MARIANIST (DIED 1967)

Father Emil Neubert wrote the first monograph, a simple article under the title *L'Union mystique à la Vierge*[97] (*Mystical Union with the Virgin*). Based on the text of its founder, he notes:

> "It is a gift of the Blessed Virgin's continual presence…which is available to those who are very faithful," and he explains it as a grace of mystical union that is free but not extraordinary (like apparitions and revelations). He does not confuse it with

the exceptional and transitory grace that Therese of Lisieux speaks of. It is a particular grace: she can "be with the souls who…will never succeed in the way of infused contemplation, but rather, most mystical souls are, it seems, never favored with it."

Father Neubert explains the essentials: "Awareness of sensing Mary, not residing in us, but acting within us by the influence of grace…with a personal touch….This is precisely what the 'gift of Mary's presence' seems to be."

He considers various aspects of this grace: identification, contemplation, and union with God himself. Finally, he finishes as he started, by emphasizing that this grace, so freely given, can be prepared for, according to Chaminade, by "very great faithfulness" (p. 28). A short time before he died, he returned to this question in his book *La Vie d'union à Marie*[98] (*Life of Union with Mary*).

DENIS BUZY (DIED 1937)

On July 13, 1937, the very Reverend Father Denis Buzy, Superior General of the Priests of the Sacred Heart, preached on Mary's presence in his hometown, at the sanctuary of Bétharram, at the request of Canon Théas, future Bishop of Lourdes, then director at the seminary in Bayonne, during the pilgrimage for the subdeacons and young priests of the seminary. This homily was deeply impressive. It was the catalyst for awareness on the subject. Abbot Théas asked Father Buzy to publish his speech.

He became uneasy. There might be criticisms against his unusual use of words. Bishop Théas answered the objection: "We have with us Blessed Grignion de Montfort, all spiritual people and even the theologians."[99] The sermon was printed under the title *La Présence de Marie dans les âmes* (*Mary's Presence in Souls*), Bayonne, 1937 (8 pages). It is a warm and poetic explanation from which emerge the following statements:

The great sacrament of Marian piety...*magnum pietatis sacramentum* is what Blessed Grignion de Montfort called the secret of Mary....For a priest, the secret of holiness is the presence of Mary in our souls. (Opening Statement)

The "presence of Mary" is not like the "physical atmosphere of Marian piety," that you breathe in at Lourdes or Bétharram; nor is it a "bodily" or sacramental presence, like that of Jesus in the Eucharist.

It is still a real presence, through its impact, and through the sanctifying grace and the uninterrupted flow of actual graces that come to us from Mary. (p. 3...)

If we can feel within ourselves the impact of Mary...we are in possession of the source of that grace. (p. 5)

But everything that comes from Mary, "you owe to Jesus." According to their perfect union, he ascribes to her everything that is due first and foremost to Jesus Christ, thus emphasizing the continuing influence of Mary "from cradle to grave." (p. 6)

REGINALD GARRIGOU-LAGRANGE († 1964)

Father Reginald Garrigou-Lagrange raises this question prominently in his book *La Mère du Sauveur et notre vie intérieure* (*The Mother of the Savior and Our Inner Life*),[100] which is intended to be a statement on the great doctrines of Mariology and how they impact our inner life. This early-twentieth-century Thomist had the merit of establishing a link between abstract thinking and his spiritual life. At the end of his career, he began showing that his adherence to theological theses concerning Mary consisted of three phases:

1. He accepted them first because they were beautiful.
2. He then grappled with the difficulties of a dual positive and speculative point of view.
3. Again he accepted them, not only because they are beautiful, "but because they are true."

These three phases are together like devotion that touches our feelings, along with dryness and "perfect spiritual devotion that washes over our feelings."

The book examines in turn the grace of Mary (her divine motherhood and fullness of grace, p. 3–173), then her mediation and her universal queenship (p. 174–297), before considering the implications of these mystical doctrines. In the chapter on mediation, a four-page note analyzes the Blessed Virgin's mode of presence in the souls that are united to her. Garrigou-Lagrange gives two possible explanations of her presence. The first is virtual or dynamic contact (p. 251–53): God would use Mary, just as he uses Christ's humanity and his union with her, as an instrumental cause, and we could speak of a "physical influence," however without her affecting us other than as a virtual contact (p. 253). He remains unsure about the validity of this explanation and only suggests it hypothetically, before giving the second explanation, which is certain—actual proof.

While the Blessed Virgin may not physically be the instrumental cause of the graces we receive, she has an "affective presence" within us as the person who is known or loved by those who love her, and at very different degrees of intimacy according to the depth and strength of our love (p. 254). He rightly emphasizes this dimension of love:

> Love, as Dionysius says, is an intuitive strength. There are two possible unions between those who love each other:

1. A real union when they are actually present to each other (like two people who are in the same place and who can see each other nearby).
2. An affective union, such as that between two people who are, physically, widely separated from each other. Each has knowledge of and love for the other person.[101]

The status of spiritual love on earth implies a distance, a journey that makes man a *Viator*. The distance does not prevent a greater perfection of emotional union, in the following two ways:

1. *Amantum est in amante*: the beloved person is within the one who loves, through the kindness that she inspires in him.
2. *Amans est in amato*: the person who loves is within the beloved, as he very powerfully and intimately welcomes what makes that person happy. So, it is a self-less happiness, strong enough to produce an "ecstasy" in which one who loves, as it were, comes out of himself, because he wants the good of his friend as his own and forgets himself; the intimacy of this union of love and presence, which are not bodily but emotional, "is a foretaste of the actual union which we will enjoy in heaven."

Here below, there are those who, like a prelude, are under the physical influence of the humanity of Jesus, and probably of the Blessed Virgin, who sent us a still greater grace and a charity that is always rooted more intimately in our will (p. 255).

Chapter 6 on "True Devotion to the Blessed Virgin" is in four sections (veneration of saints, the Rosary, consecration according to Grignion de Montfort, and mystical union with Mary), and concludes with the title and Father

Neubert's dossier, which in 1937, began this line of current thinking.

Garrigou-Lagrange sees in the mystical union a source of humility, confidence, pure love, and the transformation of the soul. He ends with the life of union "experienced by Mary of St. Teresa," the Flemish mystic.

> Many holy souls here below have, in a painful way, a deep and very invigorating intimacy with Mary, of which they do not have the opportunity to speak. For many of these souls, there is a very specific provision, an impulse to Mary, a gaze followed by her felt presence, sometimes only for a moment, like a mother who looks in at the room where her children are, to see if they are doing their homework. She then communicates ineffable piety, inspires more generous sacrifices, and a baring of oneself that enriches and allows one to enter into the depths of the *Magnificat* and also the *Stabat Mater*. (p. 334)

The author of the *Stabat* bears witness to this experience of intimacy, says Garrigou-Lagrange, and this explains the insistent repetition of the imperative *fac*:

> *Fac ut tecum lugeam*
> *Fac ut avidea cor meum*
> *Fac ut portem Christi mortem*
> *Fac me plagis vulnerari*
> *Fac me cruce inebriari et cruore Filii*
> *Fac me tecum pie flere...crucifixi condelere, donec ego vixero.*

It is here, he states, that we can grasp the profound relationship between Mariology and the inner life. The importance of this book is that it is spiritual experience that characterizes it. It inspires comments like this:

The more love is selfless and strong and intimate at the same time, the more the second aspect (*amans in amato*) tends to prevail (over the first aspect: *amantum in amante*). Then the soul is more in God than God is in the soul, and there is something similar with regard to the humanity of Jesus and the Blessed Virgin.

And this is how he views "the ecstasy of love." The issue of instrumental causality is more debatable. But Garrigou-Lagrange himself felt that it was hypothetical. It has the merit of not applying this scheme materially, but, in agreement with Saint Thomas, of rectifying the physical notion of instrumental causality, in order to locate it, more mysteriously and hypothetically, within the spiritual realm where Christ's body and Mary's body dwell (in Saint Paul's words, these are glorious bodies and spiritual bodies). He puts forward this speculative explanation while completely aware of how relative it is.

PIERRE-MARIE THÉAS (DIED 1950)

Bishop Pierre-Marie Théas, who had invited Father Buzy to publish his preaching on the presence of Mary in 1937, suggested this theme more than once to Lourdes pilgrims, without going into an elaborate study.

All the devotees of Lourdes are offered the grace of intimacy with Mary. To benefit, you must first pay attention to the sweet presence of the Virgin Mary.[102]

Although she is immersed in the splendor of the heavenly Jerusalem, Our Lady is not absent from the earth. She is present; not in a physical or quantitative way, but by her continual action, by influencing all instants that exercise her motherhood of grace....

We believe that our Mother is present to us, through all the graces, along with her divine Son, she spreads in souls and in the Church.[103]

In his book, *Ce que croyait Bernadette* (*What Bernadette Believed*),[104] he develops this theme about Bernadette's response to Sister Duray, who invited her to paint a picture of the Virgin:

> "I have no need to..., I have her in my heart."
> Mary's presence is not physical or quantitative. It is a presence of influence....This presence, this action of Mary we can perceive through faith or the feelings....We can only really know the Virgin in her relationship with the Holy Spirit.[105]

H. LEFRANC (DIED 1953)

Father H. Lefranc, MIC (superior of the College of Garaison), was attracted to this theme after a retreat preached by Father Buzy in 1948. It was a development of his preaching at Betharram in 1937. Father Lefranc was also struck by the testimony of Father Sarthe, from Garaison, who had just died. One of the sanatorium patients from Arrens where he was being treated had submitted notes on the Virgin Mary in which he said: "We have a mother who cares for us up there."

Father Sarthe corrected him: "Why up there? She is close to us, here below: very close to us...within us.... Mary is present because God is present."[106]

Father H. Lefranc[107] published his article "*Présence mariale* (Mary's Presence)" in *Unum Sint*, the Congregation's Bulletin. He refers to this experience, and he writes: "Does Mary's presence not mean anything for us? This is possible. But this only proves that we have not yet experienced, in our small way, the presence of the Blessed Virgin in our own life. We have not had this shock, this grace....The secret has remained hidden to us."[108] He wrote this study to clarify the meaning of certain terms, to allow this experience to give rise to a broader collection of texts and give a reason for Mary's presence: "Methods and Consequences."

At the end of his collection of texts (No. 9, pp. 311–18), he excludes the eucharistic and bodily presence, which Gerson seemed to lean toward (p. 342), and distinguishes three modes of Mary's presence:

1. Presence of vision: Mary sees us in God and, in a unique characteristic of the Mother of Jesus and of our souls, her knowledge penetrates to our innermost being.
2. Presence of action: Mary acts, constantly influencing us. She also acts *through* us.
3. Presence of mystical union, emotional presence (according to Father Garrigou-Lagrange): within the soul that is in a state of grace a state of supernatural love is created, involving a mystical presence with Our Lord and Mary, by which, according to theologians and the masters of the spiritual life, the person who loves is present within the person loved, and vice versa.

There then follows an attempt to establish this three-part presence along classic theological lines. The Blessed Virgin sees us very clearly in God:

- Because she is the Mother of God (p. 345).
- Because Mary is the Mother of humankind (p. 346).

The article, which ends on page 352, with the words "to be continued," remains unfinished. But the part that is published provides the substance of the matter. The theological considerations only provide a commentary drawn from conventional views of Mariology.

SEVERINO RAGAZZINI (DIED 1960)

Father Severino Ragazzini, OFM Conv., has published the most complete study on the subject.[109] Its main interest for us is to have collected a record of seventy authors to whom Ragazzini gives a useful bibliography at the beginning of his book (p. 34–40).

These are exclusively Latin authors: one father of the Church, Saint Augustine, who is hardly topical in this area, nine authors from the Middle Ages, and the other half of the list is provided by authors from the nineteenth and twentieth centuries.

With three exceptions, all authors marked with one or two asterisks (that is to say those who have been used as a topical source for the book) occur after the early seventeenth century, and among these three, Jean Cross has not developed a Marian spirituality. These texts have been chosen using no apparent criteria and in a way that is not at all obvious.

The same study of the most representative authors invites us not to generalize on the existence of Mary's presence in their lives. This presence includes periods of darkness, which must not be overlooked, especially at the endpoint, which is the mystical marriage of Saint Thérèse. It will therefore be necessary to distinguish the reality of the relationship with Mary and the feeling of her presence in the hazards of awareness and sensitivity, especially in the night of faith.

The author examines the role of Mary in the spiritual life in two parts symmetrically divided into sections, each of which itself is divided into two chapters:

1. Doctrine.
2. Experience of Mary in the various stages of the spiritual life:
   Ascetic life: active purification

> Mystical life: passive purgation, illumination and transforming union (spiritual marriage).

For every aspect and stage, he cites relevant spiritual texts. This book, like the list of sources, is limited by its structure.

The doctrine, which is simple and straightforward, encompasses these four points: "The Madonna is our mother (*mia mamma*), she is Coredemptrix, Mediatrix, and mother of the earth" (mother is the most beautiful word in the world, he says at the beginning of this chapter, p. 68). He attempts to show here that Mary gives birth to us spiritually, more than our earthly mother gave birth to us physically. This scheme owes more to the contemplative and oratorical considerations than to specific theological foundations, but it contains penetrating observations. The second section unfolds according to a framework of classical mysticism.

This makes us ask how relevant these frameworks are today with the following questions: How much does culture play a part in the development of the mystical journey? And, is spiritual progress not graduated according to knowledge rather than according to love, which is more difficult to observe, but more important?

The texts widely quoted in order to illustrate each step of the spiritual journey are not very clear and are sometimes "artificial"; so several critics have observed.[110] This book is a strong testimony to spiritual life, on the place of Mary in the Christian mystery, but it is brilliantly constructed based on theology or even on a rigorous induction taken from an interesting anthology of texts. It has double merit. This is the most documented book on the subject, the only one that attempts to demonstrate the permanence and the nature of Mary's role throughout the stages of the spiritual life.

This line of studies and explanations seems to have died with him. However, S. de Fiores took up the question again in a book called *Maria, presenza viva nel popolo di Dio*,[111] where he attempts to capture aspects of the presence of Mary in the Church's life and especially in popular religion—a perspective that is quite different from that of Ragazzini.

G. Ogioni characterizes this presence as "supratemporal," that is to say, transcending time and space. He also characterizes this presence as "pneumatic," that is to say, spiritual and related to the Spirit in the expression of the communion of saints found in 1 Corinthians.

V

WHAT PRESENCE?

DOCTRINAL AND SPIRITUAL STUDIES

It remains for us, then, to discern the foundations, nature, character, and timing of the presence of Mary; to briefly evaluate and point out where these occur.

WHY DO WE SPEAK OF PRESENCE?

A FACT

That Mary, Mother of Christ, who introduced and shared the life of Christ, is now in glory, is a given of our faith. That she is present to us in the Communion of Saints, in the unity of the Body of Christ, is an implicit fact of revelation. We are one in Christ, established in a communicative solidarity of grace. From the outset, she is the closest to Christ in terms of nature and grace, deified by the Word that she humanizes. In the tragic rupture of his death, Christ invited her to become the mother of the disciples, his brothers, which further emphasizes her solidarity with the Redeemer and with us.

THE TIMING OF THIS CONCEPT

How can we evaluate this link? To describe the role of Mary in the work of salvation, Mariology used a number of concepts that have created many distinct chapters: mediation, coredemption, queenship, spiritual motherhood, intercession, and so on. All relate differently to one problem: Mary's participation in the redemptive work of Christ, and therefore her relationship to humanity today. No dogma has yet been drawn up covering this area, despite ardent campaigns by the Marian movement, which has defined mediation, coredemption, queenship, and spiritual motherhood. Over three hundred bishops requested it again in their preferences that were sent during the preparatory phase before Vatican II. But Vatican II did not uphold this hypothesis.

A definition of faith does not seem useful in this vital but still vague matter. Rather what is required is to discern, refresh, and internalize the role of Mary in the Communion of Saints. Mary's presence has advantages in relation to these concepts:

1. Most err on the side of abstraction and ambiguity, or risk making Mary a kind of duplicate of Christ (mediation, coredemption), or tend toward a certain particularism (queenship is not without risks in this regard).
2. Most of these concepts require, sometimes very subtle, modifications.

This is why Pius XII, during his pontificate, gradually abandoned the title *mediatrix*, out of respect for the formula of the Apostle Paul referring to Christ as "sole mediator" (1 Tim 2:5).

Can Mary be called universal mediatrix of all graces of the Old Testament? Or of continual grace, which is humanity's direct actuation by divine life? These questions exercised the minds of the theologians of the Holy Office, who were consulted on the preparation of a possible definition. Can we call Mary mediatrix with Christ, the sole mediator? Or should we say that she is only participating in the mediation of Christ—"mediator in Christ," after the remarkable adjustment proposed by the Protestant Hans

Asmussen? Can we, along with the Greek homilists, refer to Mary's human mediation, at the point when she gives her consent to the incarnation of the Son of God (Luke 1:38), on behalf of all humanity?

The use of the title *mediatrix* was one of the thorniest problems that were discussed by the Council; some wanted Vatican II to teach this doctrine. Cardinal Bea wanted the Church to refrain from using this word. In order to reconcile the dispute, Vatican II finally decided to mention this title along with others, without formally teaching on it or explaining it, and to show its relativity by insistently referring to Christ as the one mediator. To take this title as the center of synthesis, in fact, would be to engage in a difficult and ambiguous theological course that does not lend itself to wide disclosure. At a time when Catholic preaching referred to Mary as mediatrix with such fervor and frequency, it was surprising to see at what point the Christian people ignored the fact that Jesus was the mediator.

The problem of spiritual motherhood, which seemed clearer, proved no less difficult. Indeed, Mary is not called Mother of God and mother of men in the same sense. The conciliar text first used the term *Mother of God*, and some raised this objection: "The word Mother does not have the same meaning when it applies to God and when it applies to men. Mary is Mother of Christ for having given birth bodily, as other mothers do. She is the mother of men (each generated by a different mother), in a spiritual and adoptive way." To resolve this ambiguity, the conciliar text was corrected. It twice repeated the word *mother* in order to uphold the diversity of meaning: "*Mother* of God and *mother* of men." The Council did not go into the background of the problem and did not specify the difference in meaning or the problems caused by the shortcut that some Popes dared to use: "Mother of God, therefore mother of humankind." The "therefore" is part of a second mission, which is accomplished in Mary through a period fraught with challenges. Jesus gives meaning to this and marks its fulfillment by his words spoken at Calvary: "Behold your Mother."

Similarly, the queenship of Mary, just like the kingship of Christ, has nothing to do with the royalties of this world. Matthew and Luke encompass this radical change in the infancy narratives in their Gospels. When it is God who becomes king, this is done with a break in the male genealogy dynasties (Joseph, son of David, is not Jesus' father) and in the most radical humility and poverty, as far as possible from palaces and political power. In contrast, "the presence of Mary" says something simple and obvious, concrete and existential, close to life. This expression connotes both mutual knowledge and action or influence that can be evaluated and qualified without narrowness of meaning or conceptual reductions.

Finally, "the presence of Mary" is not only an objective fact, but a life experience. This simple notion of presence, which is organically linked to the presence of God and in him to the Communion of Saints, allows us to reconsider, rectify, and locate the ponderous and sometimes controversial titles given pride of place by the Mariology of the Counter-Reformation. This kind of vocabulary certainly has ecumenical benefits. It is more acceptable than what went before. It belongs to the Orthodox, since it is in the East that we find the first explicit evidence of Mary's presence. The Protestant side is not without problems. In reaction against the improper worship of saints in the sixteenth century, their theology tends to reduce the Communion of Saints to the Christians of this world only, as seen by the Apostle Paul. Our relationship with the saints of the Church Triumphant is a more delicate ecumenical problem. But this is a rather difficult historical heritage. This theme is not entirely resistant to ecumenical dialogue, but we must remain attentive to the problematic and psychological difficulties; and also the tact that is very important for fruitful ecumenical dialogue.

What remains is for us to clarify the nature of her presence, what form it takes, and how to cultivate (or acquire) it.

FEELING OR FAITH?

EXPERIENCE

A superficial read through of our list of texts may give the impression that Mary's presence is a feeling. In fact, we find this word recurring in several writers or mystics. But is this presence a matter of feelings or of faith?

Looking at the text more closely, we find that the feeling (which has its place) is an epiphenomenon and not the substance of that experience. Mystics often use the word *feel* to describe this presence, which is invisible—it is not a matter of vision, but of experience. The word *sentire* is synonymous with the Latin *experiri*; it means "an experience that is not necessarily a sensory experience." The word can mean "having a sense of"; the assurance of an influence that is not seen except by its effects in the longer term. Is this not what Father Cestac wanted to express when he said: "I do not see her, but I sense her presence, like a horse senses the hand of the rider who guides it"?

This feeling or experience does not normally mean an immediate intuition. This presence is perceived by means of signs, it being understood that the sign is not a screen, but a living and transparent link through which we reach the same reality; hence the use of various signs to express or cultivate links with Mary in the Communion of Saints: scapulars, medals, badges, beads, installing icons, and, in a more intimate way, forming our own inner icon of Mary.

In short, the presence of Mary is not a vision; it is an experience of proximity, influence, maternal support, and assistance. Through these intimate and discreet signs, we see that Mary is there, right there, and that we are not abandoned. A number of witnesses attest to a more or less intense awareness of her presence, perceived or felt as close or intimate (in itself or through its effects), and a source of peace or of spiritual fruits.

FOUNDATIONS

This presence of Mary in our lives is based on the information we obtain from faith. We find that information (about this same notion of presence) by assessing Mary's presence in Scripture, in the liturgy, and in the life of local churches, before we examine our own experience, or the awareness of this presence by mystics or, more generally, by the people of God; this experience can be popular or mystical, and we should not evaluate these two categories differently. The way in which the Christian people experiences the sense of Mary's presence, her gaze, her protection, her action, can be of greater value than that of mystical writers who have the facility of expressing themselves here on earth. The quality of language does not necessarily reflect that of presence.

The four-part assessment of the aspects of Mary's presence in the source and in the life of faith leads to a very simple truth. Her presence has similar characteristics and proportions: (1) In the life of Christ and in Scripture; (2) In Christian liturgy; (3) In the life of the Church (practices, iconography, experience, protection); and (4) In the lives of Christians. In living out our life of faith, we find that what is recorded in the Gospel and in the prayer of the Church has the same universal characteristics, and also the same identity. But before specifying what these characteristics are, we must consider their theological foundations.

We will make no headway if we begin from the standpoint of the specific theses that Mariology has developed and which are so often questionable and overly particular.

The presence of Mary is drawn from more basic data. Mary is the creature who is closest to God, through her physical and spiritual (theological) ties with Christ. Sin has not darkened, nor diverted, this relationship. She is the recipient par excellence of the grace of the New Testament. The new covenant begins with Mary's informed, immediate, and full consent to Christ (Luke 1:38). This is what the name *Kecharitomene* that God (and the Scripture, Luke 1:28) has given her means: "she who has found grace," as Luke 1:30 confirms. She is also the one who was able to thank God for this gift (Luke 1:46–55).

This unrivaled presence before God is realized in Christ, through his participation in the incarnation, in a way that is free, dynamic, and active, as we see from Luke 1:28, 55. This new relationship with God is from the beginning a relationship of faith, love, and service. She inaugurates the relationship, which then continues in the mystical body. Mary is the prototype of the relationship with the Savior, Son of God, by the sign of her physical body and the theological link (through faith, hope, and charity), which is the foundation of the mystical body. In this body, which began mystically at the incarnation, we are one living being in Christ, and Mary is in first place, as a founder and prototype. The reality of the Communion of Saints begins at the annunciation.

It is she who began this wonderful exchange between the God made man and deified humankind through the pure gift of God. It is in Mary that participation began in the trinitarian community that the Gospel of John expresses by saying: "We are in Christ and Christ is in us as the Father is in the Son and the Son in the father" (John 17:21, 23). It is Mary who begins this extension of the trinitarian perichoresis in human persons created by God in his image.

She remains at the center of this solidarity in Christ, because the presence of God, as given in Christianity, is inseparable from the presence of the Incarnate Word. In this mystery, which was accomplished through the cross and through Pentecost where she was present, Mary remains willing, responsive, and cooperative. She holds a place that was hers from the start: dynamic, tangible, and living. It is important to recognize her presence, just as it is important to recognize the presence of the Lord in all of our fellow human beings, especially in the poorest. Mary is present at the beginning and at the current and historical foundations of salvation, but also at the end, in anticipating the glory that she bears witness to as an eschatological icon of the Church.

In short, the presence of Mary tells us who she is by vocation and by God's grace, a stakeholder in the initial mystery of salvation and in all the subsequent organic growth in which she took a knowing part. Her presence at the origin and birth, childhood and growth of Christ, at the first miracle of his public life and its conclusion on Calvary, at the outpouring of the Spirit and the founding of the Church, testifies to the living continuity and the universality of her presence.

We form our own personal and irreplaceable icon, our living link with Mary. This inner icon is a living sign of her presence, an expression of a lived experience that the Church recognizes. These signs nourish and refresh her presence in a way that always refers to God and Christ. This experience is grace and gift. That is why mystical theology speaks of an infused presence, that is to say, given within oneself; God giving both the awakening of the inner sign, which is formed in our psyche, and the presence itself that is realized by that sign.

All of this speaks to the fundamental condition of human knowledge, according to its humble status, as God knows. A human being is a rational animal, not an angel. We are not directly capable of intuition. We know only through *signs*. These signs are not a screen. They do not separate us from reality. On the contrary, they open us to it. Saint Thomas Aquinas expressed it so well when he said: "Faith does not end with concepts (or images), but with the reality itself that the concept (or image) signifies."[1]

This is the sense in which we say that Mary's presence is a matter of faith (and not of feelings). What it does is make real in our lives what we know through the revelation of God. This revelation, which is expressed by various signs of the Church, is given to be lived out in all its dimensions; the main aspect is the presence of God himself, the foundation of all others. It is in Him, through Him, and with Him that we are given the presence of our brothers and sisters in the Communion of Saints, those on earth and those of heaven, including Mary. This is a fundamental given that emerges from our study. Our task today, which is designed to bring God to the world, to bring about the coming of God among humanity, comes out of this divine–human solidarity.

THE CHARACTERISTICS OF MARY'S PRESENCE

IT IS DIFFERENT FROM GOD'S PRESENCE

It is important to note the differences between the presence of God and that of Mary. The presence of God is deeper, more basic, it is the principle itself of Mary's presence—its place, its divine nature. This observation is quite fundamental:

> The presence of God is the presence of the Creator. God causes us to live. He is the life principle of our existence, more intimate than we are to ourselves. If God stopped wanting us to exist (which is not conceivable, because God is faithful and constant in his actions), we would cease to exist, like an electric light goes out as soon as the current no longer

flows. This is only a comparison. God's creative power is much more fundamental. It is the first cause, underlying any secondary causes; it raises us up and penetrates us. His presence is of the order of being and not of appearance (except for miraculous manifestations).

Mary's presence is not of this order. She is not the creator but a creature. The world existed before she existed. If she stopped thinking about us, we would not cease to exist. She is not the one who causes us to exist. She is created by God, and can only cooperate with God in our wellbeing or advancement.

God's presence is not only that of the Creator. It also has its source in grace and it gives us access to the very life of God.

His presence is much more fundamental than decadent theology stated, according to which grace (whether for the moment or even continuously) was presented as a thing: a kind of object placed by God in the soul, which Mary could transmit, according to her usual role as mediator. But Scripture and Tradition describe grace as God's gift, the life of God himself. According to John 7:38–39 (cf. 4:10, 14), Jesus sends the Spirit as the source of living water welling up deep within the believer ("from his heart shall flow rivers of living water;" he means the Spirit that believers should receive).

What we must concede to the classical theology of grace is that the immediate presence of God involves a created aspect, a change in the human person. Saint Thomas Aquinas established this conclusion by saying that, because God is immutable, the newness implied by the gift of grace does not change God, but rather the creature that God visits. God's influence is imprinted on the human person. But this created aspect is only the effect of grace, of the divine life that he has communicated. It is only the root and the point of attachment. Grace is essentially, as Father de la Taille has previously recalled, the actualization of our soul by God himself, the life of God communicated and spread.

In other words, God passes his divine life of love and knowledge to us. He allows us to know him (sometimes darkly, through witnesses and signs) as he knows himself, through faith; to love him as he loves himself, through charity. Grace is a new creation: the re-creation of our lives by God, who gives us a share in his life, according to our measure, because he plumbs the depth of the infinite and the eternal. This is one of the deepest secrets of human destiny. The supernatural is not an external addition—like a hat on a head—but an impulse, a deep desire that God has placed in us to fulfill ourselves in him.

Mary's presence is not of this type. She is not, like the Father, the Son, and the Holy Spirit, the divine principle of grace, the source of divine life, through which she also receives God. She is not the author of the new creation, but a servant of the Lord. God alone passes his own life to us, directly. And this immediacy (the direct character of God's gift) has always been the major objection to the theory of universal mediation. How can Mary be the mediatrix of this direct relationship with God? Other words would therefore be best to describe her ineffable role in helping us to receive and accept this divine presence, in which she is so immersed.

MARY'S PRESENCE IN GOD, AND IN CHRIST

Consequently, Mary's presence is in God and through God. This is how the mystics perceive it, as a bright light or more discreetly, as appropriate. For them she is always inseparable from God, like a stream from that source. Mary's presence is therefore not a creative presence. It is a moral presence of knowledge and love, example and influence. If we know and admire her as the perfect image of God, we learn to imitate her love for her children, just as all love tends to act and communicate.

How does she communicate? It is here that theologians grope for words and the best of them, including Garrigou-Lagrange, find themselves at a loss. Symbolic images, which abounded in the theology of mediation, are merely approximations. They cannot be taken literally in that they represent Mary using a mechanical model, such as a canal or aqueduct by which grace is sent to us. These images were meant to explain Mary's influence, closely linked to that of God. They do not tell us the secret of how this is achieved.

We should say something about the different theories that have been developed to account for it. We obviously do not give in to the temptation of finding a physical presence of Mary in the Eucharist; that is a false trail that was sometimes pursued and that seems to haunt Gerson himself. Attempts to find her presence through a particle of her body persisting in the body of Christ, or any other explanation like this, are obviously ridiculous. Three theories that should be considered are:

1. Instrumental causality
2. Dispositive causality
3. Inclusion in the network of interpersonal relations

The notion of instrumental cause has the advantage of dealing with two important truths. First, God's role is always primary. And second, Mary's role is subordinate— everything that comes to us from her comes first and most essentially from God himself, who imbues her being, her freedom, her grace, and even her influence. She is a sign through which God reveals himself.

But if we want to speak about **instrumental causality**, we must purify this concept. Mary is not like a tool the carpenter holds in his hand. She is not an object. When God awakens human freedom, it is a freedom to be, and God respects that freedom infinitely better than any human being who uses another, albeit with much love and respect. The active presence of Mary is something more intimate, profound, ineffable, which is expressed using the model of instrumental causality.

In order to avoid the emerging risks of using such an approximate concept, we tried to define the role of Mary as a **dispositive causality**. This concept expresses well that Mary does not give what essentially comes directly from God, but prepares and disposes the receiver. By his example and influence, she prompts the dispositions that allow us to receive God's action, to internalize it better. This pattern reflects just an aspect of Mary's role. But I do not think we need to generalize or systematize it here.

Our relationship with Mary in God is a mystery that we can identify, locate, but not adequately express. Let us not reduce the realities of faith to mere theories. We can identify the role of Mary more modestly by assessing her place in the existential aspect of **interpersonal relationships**. In the communication that the three divine persons established with humanity, Mary takes first place, as having the most intimacy with God, and the most solidarity with humanity. In the interpersonal network of these relationships, she holds the highest position; after Christ God and man, who is the basis of these relations, she has the most intense and most communicative role.

This is the key to these relationships, according to Saint Louis-Marie Grignion de Montfort: Mary is relative to Christ. We must perceive not a kind of relativism that would render her insignificant, but a dynamic and positive reference that defines her being and her value. Humanity's worth is in relation to God, and by returning to God, as Saint Augustine taught. And Mary, having received God's gift with the utmost readiness and without interference, was able to make a perfect return to him in thanksgiving. This is what is expressed in her *Magnificat*.

Mary's perfect relationship with God and with human-kind, whom she serves in God, is a transcendent inter-change as she comes from the three persons of the Trinity in order to lead us back to them; a personal interchange, because the person of the Father, the first principle, acts through the Son and the Spirit whom he sends to human-ity, thus completing human beings divinely—he raises their nature by sharing the same love that puts them level with him. So he converts the human impulse into agape, the desire to give; this is the essence of our re-creation, when natural selfishness is converted into altruism in the image of God.

MARY'S PERMANENT AND UNIVERSAL PRESENCE

Mary's presence is permanent and universal in the sense that nothing is outside of her grasp, as she partici-pates in the divine life at the heart of her commitment to humankind. More specifically, nothing is beyond her, nei-ther at the time of salvation, nor in the work of salvation where God has involved her from the start: the incarna-tion. Thus she is the starting point in the communion of God and humanity because by agreeing to give birth to the Son of God so that he might become the Savior, she clung to him by faith and charity. She was thus not only the first member of the mystical body, the founder member and essential part of it, but through the Holy Spirit (Luke 1:35), she gave birth to both Christ and the Church, where she did not remain the only member in a one-on-one relation-ship with the Son of God who became her son, but left in haste driven by the same spirit, so that Elizabeth, John the Baptist, and Zechariah could be filled with the Holy Spirit in their turn (Luke 1:39–46) and also the elderly Simeon and Anna at the Presentation (Luke 2:25–38). She did this out of this same love, because the ontological gap between God and Mary, his creature, did not prevent personal growth through the communication of divine love. And this is the characteristic of love: to put the greatest and the smallest on the same level, just like the king who marries a shepherdess in the tales our grandmothers told us. Moreover, love puts the king at the feet of the shepherdess and, in reality, prepares them for dedicated service to their children who demand everything of them. So God has placed in human nature a parable of his relationship with us his creatures and his children. This is what Christ demonstrated by washing the feet of his disciples. According to the cycle of love, it also invites the children to serve their elderly parents. Similarly, the washing of the feet inspired the disciples to serve Christ and his Father, unto death. Such are the paradoxes of love that should be the foundation of all theology. Love is reciprocal.

Mary, whom God has established in the summit of love in Christ, is both a point of attraction and a help, an immeasurable maternal effusion. In this way, Mary has founded the Communion of Saints, and by a very tangible link that is both human and divine.

- In human terms, she provides Christ with corporeal being, human birth, and the human education needed for the psychological awakening and growth of every person (attempts to raise children in an incubator, separated from any woman or nurse substitute, turned out to be disasters that resulted in irreversible psychological underdevelopment and often death).
- In divine terms, she received unparalleled grace to help in nurturing Jesus. God required her free consent to perform this work.

In this sense, we can apply the formula of the parable of the prodigal son to her relationship with Christ: "All that is yours is mine, what is mine is yours." The wonderful exchange of the incarnation, which the Church fathers speak of, began with Christ and Mary. If it is impossible to speak of universal mediation, in the sense of a universal intermediary, Mary is completely committed to the universality of the mystery of the incarnation and redemption, in an exemplary and irreversible manner. We are called to enter into communion in the same way that this Jewish girl from a village in Galilee is committed, at a universal level. This communion, which started in a particular time and place with the Holy Spirit, continues to build, for it extends to all. The Holy Spirit brings about the reality (*res*) while Christ is the sign and reality (*res et sacramentum*) and the Father is the root source and intimate reality (*fons divinitatis*).

MARY'S HUMAN AND FEMININE PRESENCE

Mary's presence is both human and feminine. Her humanity emphasizes that her personal, irreplaceable existence historically precedes and exceeds her maternal function. All existence is freedom, and emergence. Mary existed. God raised up within her the fundamental phenomenon of existence, which is the basis of existence for others, and of creativity. The gift of God raised Mary's personal life and dynamism to the service of salvation.

MARY'S MATERNAL PRESENCE

Mary's presence is a maternal presence. She is the Mother of Christ, the universal man because he is the God-man. She blossomed into full motherhood (fully turned toward God but also fully human), and through her new vocation (John 19:25–27), God has extended this motherhood to all humanity.

This new motherhood is adoptive. But adoption is not a second-class motherhood. For a woman, it is a joint adventure, to adopt in reality and to gain the acceptance of the adopted child. Marcel Pagnol wrote an excellent play, *Marius*, which opens with this theme: The young Marius, a citizen of the southern city of Marseille, is the lover of Fanny whom he wants to marry. But he dreams of going to sea. The call of the sea proves the stronger and he suddenly embarks on a ship, as a sailor, without leaving Fanny time to tell him she is pregnant. Panisse, an old man who secretly loved Fanny, takes her for his wife, happy to save her honor. A few months after the birth, Marius returns from his long voyage. He would like to take Fanny and the child, which is his. Panisse, the old man, can argue that he is the real father:

> You gave life, of course, he said, in essence. But even dogs do that. If I had not been there, that child would be a little bastard, to his shame. I gave him a name, a cradle, a house, and good repute. When he was born, he weighed only six pounds, and now he weighs more than twenty pounds. These are twenty pounds of love!

Panisse has no doubt that he became the father that Marius was not, because he loved unconditionally while Marius did not—he only had a semblance of superficial love. He sacrificed Fanny and her child to his craving to travel. The experience of adoptive motherhood is a profound experience. It engages all the resources of the mother's heart.

A childless woman I knew, along with her husband, decided to adopt. Once a child had been allocated, she made several visits so that the child could get used to her.

But he clung to the orphanage nurse who cared for him. The adoptive mother was anxious. Her husband joked, "This is more important to you than our engagement!" Finally, one stormy day, there was a thunderclap and the child was afraid. This time, he took refuge in her arms spontaneously. She became his mother. It was a great moment in her life.

Another mother, who already had several children, adopted a Vietnamese child out of human and Christian concern. It was difficult. The child seemed strange. He was already four or five years old and only spoke his native language, not a word of French. He used to hide and disappear from time to time. His mother was worried and so she got in touch with a Vietnamese family so that he could play, talk, and feel comfortable. She took great pains to find the appropriate environment where he would find the cultural roots she could not give him. But when she went there, the child spoke and played only for a moment. Then he took refuge on her lap and would not let go of her. He was afraid he was going to be transferred again. He wouldn't have left her for all the world. Without knowing it, she had already become his mother. And that was how she found out.

Adoption is not an artificial motherhood, or a sham. It comes out of the depths of the human heart. It is something profound, basic, and intimate. Mary, who is the Mother of Christ bodily, just like every other mother (biologically speaking), is our adoptive mother. It is a spiritual motherhood, acquired, moral, existential, and complete on a theological level. It is a true motherhood. An adoptive mother is a real mother, not an unnatural mother. It seems to me artificial to seek in Mary some ontological mechanism for adoption, as some have. Certainly we can say that Mary has adopted us at Calvary through the pains of childbirth, at a time when her divine only son, the best of the children of men, died leaving her all of sinful humanity as a legacy. When we think of the heart, the gift, the suffering, it is a true motherhood, even though the only one to whom she gave birth on earth was Christ. And all other human beings were born of another woman, an irreplaceable role that Mary does not erase but completes. All this is only at the level of the heart, without prejudice to any other terms.

MARY'S FREE AND NONPOSSESSIVE PRESENCE

Let us be specific in order to avoid any misleading ideas: Mary is not a possessive mother. Some rather worrisome forms of piety project this artificial concept onto her: she is the jealous *genitrix*, spying, exerting pressure, chastising, manipulating our feelings. "You don't love me? Then too bad for you!"

Mary was not a possessive mother toward Jesus. She let him travel in the caravan without constantly keeping an eye on him (Luke 2:40–46). She waited a whole day before wondering where he might be. She respected his freedom. She respects the same freedom of her adopted children. She does not need to blackmail our "feelings," but instead invites us to better perceive the truth about Christ and the purpose for which he calls us before God and men.

In our time (which is characterized by the "death of the father," and an "uprising against the mother"), it is important to understand the motherhood of Mary. But it is important that we do not reduce Mary to her motherhood, since she is so important. Mary exists as a person. Her motherhood is a function that her personality precedes and goes beyond. The Holy Spirit generously takes her beyond this role, because the essence of the Holy Spirit's action, similar to the best teachers, is that it awakens us both to ourselves (to the best in ourselves) and to Christ (to our identification with Christ). Mary reflects this specific feature of the Holy Spirit.

It is also quite clear that this does not mean that we should return to the womb of Mary, as suggested by some spiritualties. The desire to return to the womb betrays a certain infantilism. However, I do not condemn this interpretation. It may even have some momentary therapeutic value for the wounded of life who need to return to the warmth they came from. But Mary is not the kind of mother who would only think of sitting her children on her lap. She wants them to live, to act, to communicate and share. If we linger in the idea of the womb, it only proves that we have to overcome a momentary infantilism. Mary does not expect us to stay in that condition. She leads us to Christ and to our adulthood.

MARY'S DISCREET PRESENCE

Generally, Mary's presence remains the same kind of presence she had with Jesus, without splendor or exuberance, and the life of the Church at the end of her life where she did not hold any hierarchical position but instead shone through her prayer, her intercession, her attention, and her memory, through which she passed on to the apostles the details of Christ's childhood that they did not know, as Pope Leo XIII pointed out.

Mary's presence, with its various manifestations, is inseparable from the presence of her Son, just as that of her Son is inseparable from the trinitarian presence of the three divine persons. This is another aspect of her discreetness. And it is explained by her most perfect identification with God himself in Christ and expresses the ultimate goal to which he led his disciples, as he asks the Father, in chapter 17 of Saint John's Gospel at the end of his final prayer after the Last Supper: "That they may all be one. As you, Father, are in me and I am in you, may they also be in us, so that the world may believe that you have sent me. The glory that you have given me I have given them, so that they may be one, as we are one, I in them and you in me."

This presence has two inseparable aspects but cannot be expressed as one because it is characterized by identification but not fusion or absorption. The unity of the divine persons is not confused. Everything is shared but each person keeps his divine personality, his differentiation, his complementarity: the Father gives everything to the Son and the Son receives everything from the Father. The Father is the principle *hierarchos*, as the Greeks say, that is to say *archei*: "the absolute beginning," while the Son is receptivity, thanksgiving, recognition, which gives back to the Father in love all that he has received. This is a relationship of contrasts. Thomas Aquinas goes on to say that their relationship is one of opposition, not in the sense that they oppose each other, but that they relate to each other in complementarity between the two persons.

Hegel and even Hans Urs von Balthasar have distorted or caricatured this opposition. Hegel said that the Son was the antithesis of the Father and that the Holy Spirit was their synthesis, according to his philosophical model: thesis, antithesis, and synthesis. The latter states it less dramatically, in speaking of the kenosis of the Father; that is to say his annihilation, as he generates the Son. You could understand it in this sense if there were a "kenosis" element to human generation. Psychoanalytical theory also provides a link between death and sexuality. There is some truth in this interpretation since, in order to give birth to the next generation which will continue on, the father and mother perpetuate the rhythm of successive generations by dying: "I have raised my children. The family is being fully promoted and multiplied, according to the precept of the Creator. I can go now like the aged Simeon."

But in God, love generated by the Father does not cause self-annihilation because the Son does not detach from him but remains in him. John 17:21 (and elsewhere) expresses this as "Him in Me and I in him," which highlights both the distinction of persons and unity through the identification of knowledge and action, life and being. And John 1:18 finally translates this inwardness by using a maternal, human image, but with the difference that the child eventually detaches from its mother at birth, then at marriage, while the Son does not detach from the Father. Their relationship is eternal, immutable, without beginning or end, and they live out their relationship begetting and being begotten. All this characterizes divine love as the essence, the absolute, and the model of all perfection to which every human being is called. Love is discreet. Perfection is discreet and is the driving principle behind all manifestations that emerge from it, but radiance is the main attribute of these manifestations. Love itself remains inexplicable, whether divine or human love, and words and phrases fail when trying to express its essence.

AN IMAGE OF TRINITARIAN LOVE

Mary is the first supreme reflection of divine love among humankind and among the angels. That is why we recognize the "Queen of Angels," not because of human supremacy and glory, but because she is the first and most intimate expression of divine love. It is this same love that is diffused in her human and feminine nature but in the most profound fullness of love.

The discretion of love does not prevent impressive and striking manifestations from existing; what characterizes Mary is the frequency of her appearances that fulfill true visionaries, and she often raises them to the highest mystical level. We must not confuse the Virgin's apparitions, which are a charism, and her personal contact.

Motherhood characterizes Mary in the Bible, according to what was prophesied or prefigured about her. Thus she is designated in the Gospel—John does not even mention her name. (If the Gospel of Luke had not emerged, we would be ignorant of it!) For him, she is the mother of Jesus (John 2:1; 19:25), and that is how Acts 1:14 presents her. But above all, the title of *mother* best describes who she is: her vocation, her mission, the main purpose of her life as Mother of God and mother of humankind. Motherhood is the crown of creation, because at the human level there is no gift greater than that of a mother to the child she creates along with God and her husband, and she has the dominant share of this gift. She gives from her body the egg, which contains all the sources of life and development; this is so marked that scientists are now experimenting, trying to bring about parthenogenesis. She maintains and feeds her child in a profound symbiosis that is both organic and psychological, and gradually becomes reciprocal on the part of the child.

Pregnancy is the most fully physical and even psychological union of all for a human being. This gift is the highest form of altruism that there is. It is more deeply and tenderly programmed in the mother than the father. She gives her whole life to the person to whom she provides the foundations of existence (and also that existence itself). This is the essence of the gift, the image of the Eternal Father, from which the Bible so often presents the transcendent fatherhood of God, as motherhood, using a wide variety of images. God said to his people: "Can a woman forget her nursing child, or show no compassion for the child of her womb? Even these may forget, yet I will not forget you." And the fourth Gospel says that the only begotten Son is "close to the Father's heart" (John 1:18).

Motherhood is the ultimate image of eternal generation. Most women actually realize all of this efficiently and naturally, although to varying degrees, and Mary does it, more than any other, without selfishness or sin. Moreover, she is the Mother of God's Son. This is a fully human motherhood, body and spirit, but incurs a transcendent and direct relationship with a divine person. God raises her love to a divine level so that she can be worthy of being the Mother of God, but without distorting or altering or caricaturing her human nature. She remains the truest, simplest, most natural, and most transparent of all women. It is difficult to imagine how transparent God was when he became a man and was born of an ordinary mother.

If, then, motherhood is the cosmic crown of creation and of humanity, divine motherhood is a masterpiece of all masterpieces to a divine level; not that Mary is God, but she identifies with God as deeply as it is possible to do in her relationship with him, a relationship that is both divine and human, which does not change, nor become distorted, nor alter human nature, since God has stamped his image on that nature, which was created in his image, and is as transcendent as love and equality, because love creates equality—supreme love and supreme equality. Mary is thus the supreme image of God, inseparable from Christ, who became man in order to save humanity. She received maternal grace not only to help us, with and in Christ, to carry within us the image of God in love, but, together with her, to promote our availability and our cooperation with God's plan to transform humanity into the identity of God (John 17:21–22).

VI

TO LIVE IN MARY'S PRESENCE

AWARENESS AND PRESENCE

The practical issue is this: Mary's presence is a fact, a given of faith. How can we develop awareness and have a fruitful and authentic experience of it? It is a gift and not a commodity that is acquired through our effort alone; like all spiritual gifts, it may be desired and asked for. We can make ourselves ready to receive it and have it grow freely. The gift and the effort (our responsiveness) normally both require each other.

So what is there about Mary's presence that depends on us? It is that her presence should be grounded theologically and recognized, in spirit and in truth, without confusion or deviation. We also retain the vivid sense of the presence of God, of Mary or the saints, through faith; but faith is subject to eclipses, with long periods of darkness and temptations, even for the greatest saints. But even if the feeling of her presence often flees from those who have experienced it intensely and have clearly seen its fruit, this is not something for them to worry about. It is a normal phenomenon, not a punishment or a reproach. It is enough for them to test and discern, without dramatizing it, whether the dryness is caused by infidelity or whether it is a trial to be undergone, even if it is severe or prolonged.

Those who have witnessed Mary's presence have sometimes noted that the happy time in which they enjoyed her living presence was only a momentary grace. Saint Thérèse of Lisieux was in the light, as though under the mantle of the Virgin, for only eight days. This exceptional period of contemplation was accompanied by an ability to carry out all her material, liturgical, and spiritual duties perfectly. She perceived this and, in the end, her destiny was a dark night of the soul in which she was tempted to atheism, which she felt so agonizingly. And Bernadette Soubirous avoided any conversation about the apparitions during the final years of her illness, so that the last investigations aroused doubts because she could not recall the profound impact of her visionary experience. We have denounced hoaxes and false mystics.

We need awareness of this presence, this gift, to flourish in trust and thanksgiving. It must be present in any such exchanges and we must cultivate its fruits, with reciprocity, without which our love is not real but is only a sterile sentiment or a distant appreciation. This is how to live:

- As a servant, without servility,
- As a son or daughter, without passive dependence,
- As sibling to this elder sister, in admiration for the exemplary, prototypical, and fundamental grace she has so beautifully taken on.

HOW DO WE CULTIVATE THIS GRACE? HOW DO WE USE IT?

We must be careful not to polarize this gift—Mary's presence may be of varying types. It is not necessary that all of life be focused on this one aspect of the Christian life. This is just one aspect among others. It is left up to Christian freedom and the variety that gives value to human life. We can say this without devaluing Mary's presence. Those who have experienced this, from Grignion de Montfort to John Paul II (who revived his motto: *Totus Tuus*), see it as one of the keys to holiness, zeal, faithfulness, effectiveness, and joy that can overcome any cross.

We must therefore be open to this presence, know how to identify the inner and outward signs, and take advantage of the opportunities that present themselves. We must discern her presence by the characteristics that we have described: a presence that is universal, maternal and fraternal, discreet, and leading to Christ, an invitation without being pressured to give of ourselves, which is one of the main fruits of this presence.

We are dealing with grace that is clear and is not given to puffing us up with pride, overburdening us, wielding excessive emotion or elaborate theology. It has nothing to do with the excesses and sentimentality that make some Marian devotion so repellent. What matters is reality. Once we understand Scripture well, we will have privileged access to Mary's presence. She manifests the importance of the word of God, in Christ, if you know to read it correctly.

If we reduce Mary to a fiction, albeit a sublime fiction, if we say that she is not a historical but a symbolic figure (as stated by Pannenberg and R. E. Brown, with various nuances), if her vocation (Luke 1:28–38) is only the fictional, mythological, and legendary construction projected by the evangelists; if Mary did not really participate freely, theologically speaking, in the incarnation and in Christ's redemptive death and if, *a fortiori*, Christ is "nothing but a man," as Mary Magdalene says in *Jesus Christ Superstar*, and as some theologians more or less imply, her presence and her existence itself disappear. How then can we discern the key points (to varying degrees) where the Lord himself has placed Mary's vocation and role? They can be identified by two criteria:

1. What are the highlights in Scripture, the liturgy, and the life of the Churches?
2. What are they in the Christian experience?

Mary's role is described with particular clarity in Scripture where there is a clear contrast, particularly pronounced in Jesus' public life, between the time when Mary is close to Jesus (actively and visibly engaged in the work of salvation) and the times of separation that we have already analyzed. Mary is the "Virgin of beginnings." She had a role as initiator and founder at the incarnation and in the infancy of Christ; at Cana, the inaugural sign of Jesus' ministry; and then in the inception of the nascent Church at Pentecost.

For us too she is the **Virgin of beginnings**. It is good to offer her all that we do, what the Lord inspires in us, and ask for her help to accomplish it. This used to be the custom of Christian mothers: they offered their child to Mary as soon as they knew they were pregnant. She, who brought about the beginning par excellence, has undertaken to help us in our beginnings, to lead them to their completion, perfection, and consummation.

Mary is the **Virgin of transitions** (and this is the same thing, because there is no beginning without having a transition). The annunciation is the beginning of the New Testament. It is also the passage from the Old Testament to the New. The Daughter of Zion foretold by the prophets became the Mother of the Lord, the first member of Christ, and the starting point for the Church in communion with Christ. The transition from the hidden life to the public life by means of the first of Christ's miracles (John 2) has the same characteristic. Similarly, Mary was right there at the transition from the time of Christ to the time of the Spirit and the Church according to Acts 1:14. So we have to entrust to Mary the transitions, crises, and difficult times in our lives, our projects, and our ministries.

She is the **Virgin of the dark night of the soul**. She has been called "Star of the Sea" since the Middle Ages— Our Lady of the *Stabat Mater*, the painful icon of Golgotha, playing her role in these painful transitions, trials, and crosses. In these times of desolation and darkness, death and darkness are not eliminated. She herself has lived through them in faith, but she brings us peace in the cross and in the night. Let us think of her when we are overwhelmed by events and by our own internal difficulties, in sickness or "at the hour of our death," as we say in the Hail Mary. She aims to assist us in our daily trials and the ultimate test of life. She is our mother at the hour of our birth into heaven.

Mary's presence is only one aspect of God's presence. There is no need for us to increase either the emotional aspect or the special graces of her presence. We need not worry about circumstances; it is normal for light and darkness to alternate. Dark nights of the soul are often a time of trial for a deepening in the faith. In many cases, the presence of Mary is also a powerful moment during which she leads us to Christ; God alone is the final goal of all spirituality. For Martin Luther, just as for Grignion de Montfort, this is arguably the keynote, the central term, the most common theme of their writing, despite the considerable differences in their lives and in their thought.

The grace of Mary's presence is free and comes in many forms; let us ask that each of us welcome it as such in the freedom of the children of God.

NOTES

CHAPTER I

1. Sermon 3 on the Salve Regina, J.-P. Migne, ed., Patrologia latina (hereafter PL), vol. 184 (Paris, 1844–64), 1079.

2. René Laurentin, *Les Évangiles de Noël*, ed. F. X. de Guibert (Paris: Desclée, 2010), 212–43.

3. René Laurentin, *Les Évangiles de l'Enfance* (Paris: Éditions Desclée, 1982), 134, 520–21.

4. All these previous prophecies are detailed in Laurentin, *Les Évangiles de Noël*.

5. Cf. Num 9:18–22; 2 Chr 5:6–7.

6. Further detail in Laurentin, *Les Évangiles de Noël*, 86–88.

7. Aristide Serra, *Contributi dell'Antica Letteratura Giudaica per l'Esegesi di Giovanni 2,1–12 E 19,25–27* (Roma: Ed. Herder,1977), 45–89.

8. F. M. Braun, OP, *La Mère des Fidèles–Essai de Théologie Johannique* (Tournai-Paris: Casterman, 1953).

9. Quote from Thomas Aquinas in *Evangelium Johannis* (Taurini: Marietti, 1919), 79, quoted by Braun, 53.

10. Alfred Resch, *Das Kindheitsevangelium*, TU 10, 5 (Leipzig: Hinrich, 1897). René Laurentin, *Structure et Théologie de Luc 1–2* (Paris: J. Gabalda, 1957), 135–39; and *Les Évangiles de l'Enfance*, 385–87; cf. 400–481.

11. The dense symbolic elements contained in the episode of the finding in the temple are covered in *Les Évangiles de l'Enfance*, 110–13.

12. This role is analyzed in ibid., 199–200.

13. Yves Congar, "Incidences Ecclésiologiques d'un Theme de Dévotion Mariale," *Mélanges de Sciences Religieuses* 7 (1950):

291–92; René Laurentin, *Marie, l'Église et le Sacerdoce*: Étude Théologique, vol. 2 (Paris: Nouvelles Éditions Latines, 1953), 138–39n20. The oldest witness is Odon d'Ourscamp, ca. 116. The theme dies away with Occam.

14. Bibliography in René Laurentin, *Court Traité sur la Vierge Marie*, 5th ed. (Paris: P. Lethielleux, 1967), 120n36.

15. *L'Église du Verbe Incarné*, vol. 1 (Paris: DDB, 1941), c. 3, p. 120, note.

16. René Laurentin, *Vie Authentique de Marie* (Paris: Éd Oeuvre, 2007), 431–56.

CHAPTER II

1. The source of Luke 1—2, which I explain in *Les Évangiles de l'Enfance.*

2. *Êgapêsen*, 7, 3, ed. Strycker, 100.

3. Translated by J. Labourt and P. Battifol (Paris: 1911); cf. *DACL* 3, 167. (NB. English translation by James H. Charlesworth, Ode 19, 6–11) (gnosis.org/library/odes.htm).

4. Milton S. Terry, *The Sibylline Oracles* (New York: Hunt A. Eaton, 1890). Translated from the Greek into English blank verse. (http://www.sacred-texts.com/cla/sib/sib10.htm)

5. *Pars eximia efficitur sacri cultus*: AAS 66 (1974), Apostolic Exhortation of His Holiness Paul VI, *Marialis Cultus*, Introduction. (http://www.vatican.va/holy_father/paul_vi/apost _exhortations/documents/hf_p-vi_exh_19740202_marialis-cul tus_en.html)

6. *Unius cultus qui iure meritoquae christianus appellatur*: where he uses the most current expression: "the place Mary has in Christian worship": *de loco tractaturis quem Beata Maria virgo in cultu christiano optinet.*

7. *De schismate donatistarum* 2, 4 (CSEL 26, p. 38).

8. *Letter 282* on the martyrdom of Hesychius.

9. "Deliver us, we beseech Thee, O Lord, from all evils, past, present, and to come; and by the intercession of the Blessed and glorious ever Virgin Mary, Mother of God, and of the holy Apostles, Peter and Paul."

10. Davide Montagna, "*La liturgia mariana primitiva*," *Marianum* 24 (1962): 89.

11. Égéria (381–384), "Journal de voyage," *Sources chrétiennes* 296 (1982): 250–51n1.

12. G. la Piana, 1909 and updated republication of D. Montagna, "*La lode alla Theotokos*," *Marianum* (1963): 98.

13. Patrologia graeca (hereafter PG) 62, 766, falsely attributed to John Chrysostom. Corrective charts of *Court Traité*, Édition 1953, 163 and D. Montagna, in *Marianum* 24 (1962): 120.

14. After 451; in *Deiparam* 2, PG 93, 1468.

15. Iaroslaus Polc, *De Origine festi Visitationis B.M.V.* (Rome: Lateranense, 1967).

16. *Panarion* 78, n. 10–11 (AD 716); PG 42, GCS 37, 461–62.

17. Published by Joseph Escola (Lerida, 1859).

18. The text is reproduced in *Revues des Sciences philosophiques et théologiques* 65 (1981): 328–30.

19. (Manchester), identified by Dom Mercenier in *Le Muséon* 52 (1939): 229–33. He recognized that this text was Greek even though up until that point it was considered to be a Latin creation of the Middle Ages.

20. Quoted by Eusebius, *Ecclesiastical History* 7, 32, PG 67, 812 AB, etc.

21. Gregory Nazianzen, *Oratio* 24, PG 35, 1180 D–1181 A, study by Jourjon in *Études mariales* 23, p. 46.

22. An important monograph on this has been left by Father Barré which is, unfortunately, unfinished and unpublished.

CHAPTER III

1. PG 65, 619; René Laurentin, *Court Traité sur la Vierge Marie* (Paris: Lethielleux, 1967), 57.

CHAPTER IV

1. PL 14, 5Lk 1:1521D.

2. PL 15, 1560C.

3. *Exposition sur l'Évangile de Luc 2, 22*; éditions Sources chrétiennes 50, 82; PL 15, 1560C; Bourassé 15, 702.

4. *De Isaac* 6, 52–53, PL 14, 521c; Bourassé 117.

5. *De Virginitate Perpetua S. Mariae*, XII, in PL 96, chap.

12; and *Santos Padres Españoles* (ed. J. C. Ruiz), BAC 320, 147–52.

6. *Sermon on the Dormition*, PG 98, 344D–345C.

7. Germanus of Constantinople was patriarch of Constantinople from 715 to 730, before being driven out by Emperor Leo the Isaurian, the iconoclast.

8. *Sermon 2 on the Dormition*, no. 19, PG 96, 752BCD.

9. 96, 721AB, conclusion.

10. Edited by A. Wenger, in *Revue d'Études Byzantines* 16 (1958): 53, 58.

11. *Canticle 77, 15, Works*, ed. Seuil, 1318.

12. Spiritual motherhood often suggests certain representations of Mary's presence: as a mother holding the child in her arms, enclosed in her cloak, or even shown in her womb. The latter image does, however, run the risk of sounding a little child-obsessed. It is not essential to spiritual motherhood. Being a mother does not involve possessing the child, but rather from the outset, bringing the child into the world and awakening that child to its own life, to its own personality. The true maternal bond respects the freedom and autonomy of the child.

13. PL 101, 749B; quoted in Bourassé 3 (1579).

14. Manuscript in the Bibliothèque Nationale de France, new Latin acquisitions 186, ed J. Leclercq, in *Éphémérides Liturgicae* 72 (1958): 303.

15. PL 188, 1342B.

16. *Super Stabat*, John 19:25–27, p. 244, transcript by H. Barré in *Études Mariales* 16 (1959): 110.

17. Odon of Morimont, *Ms Munich* 281 89, p. 254.

18. Ibid.

19. *Traité de la Vraie Dévotion*, nos. 98–99, Éd. Seuil, 551.

20. Odon of Morimont, *Ms Munich* 281 89, p. 254.

21. Published in Dreves 1, no. 103, p. 108B, lines 51–53.

22. *Sermon 3, In Laudem Mariae for the 3rd Sunday in Lent, Opera 1*, p. 163, 3–7.

23. Élisée de la Nativité, OCD, *La Vie Mariale au Carmel in Maria 2*, 843–45, which reappears in *Vies de Saint Pierre Thomas* by Jean Carmesson, OFM, in *Speculum Carmelitatum*, no. 620 and by Abbot Parraud (Avignon: 1895).

24. Wadding (Lyon, 1637).

25. Text quoted by Girard, *Vie d'Union à Marie*, 180; and P. M. Théas, *Au Ciel*, in *Journal de la Grotte de Lourdes* 110, no. 16 (1961), in reference to *Livre d'or Édité at Louvain*, 432.

26. Élisée de la Nativité, OCD, in *Maria 2*, 849.

27. Ibid., 849–50.

28. Saint Francis de Sales in *Maria 2*, 994–95.

29. *Letter 312*, in the edition quoted by C. Flachaire, *La Dévotion à la Vierge*, at the beginning of the seventeenth century (Paris, 1916), 35.

30. (1) the text on *Marian Life* was published in two editions: Flemish at Malines in 1669, and Latin at Amberes in 1671. Texts regarding Mary are contained in the fourth book of the *Treatise on Godly Life*. It was reprinted and translated many times from 1926:

• *Introductio ad Vitam Internam et Fruitiva Praxis Vitae Mysticae*, edited by Gabriel Wessels O. Carm (Roma, 1926), where the treatise *De Vita Mariae Formi et Mariani in Maria et Propter Mariam* was published in an appendix.

• Élie Banon, O. Carm, *Introduction a la Vida Interna y Practica Fruitiva de la Vida Mistica* (Barcelona: Editorial Vilamala, 1936): Spanish translation of the previous edition.

• *Treatise on Mariform and Marian Life, Tratactus de Vita Mariaeformi et Mariana in Mari et Propter Mariam*, Latin text and French translation *Vie Carmélitaine* 16 (April 1931): 221–40; and (October 1931), chap. 8—13, 217–325.

• Spanish translation in Miguel de San Augustin's *La Vida de Union con Maria* (Madrid: Rialo, 1957), 37–85.

(2) *Vie de la Vénérable Mère Marie de Sainte Thérèse*, Ghent, 1683–84, 2 volumes in which his spiritual director publishes his spiritual sayings, letters, and notes. There were many partial responses to these from 1928 to 1957:

• *La Vie Mariale*, extracts translated by L. Van den Bossche in *Vie Spirituelle* 17 (1928): 204–41.

• *De la Vie Marie-Forme au Mariage Mystique*, Flemish text, translation and introduction by L. Van den Bossche in *Études Carmélitaines* 16 (October 1931): chap. 1—5, 236–50; and 17 (April 1932): ch. 6—16, 279–94 (Flemish text with French translation).

- *Vie Mariale*, fragments translated by L. Van den Bossche (Bruges, Paris, 1928).
- *L'Union Mystique à Marie, Cahiers de la Vierge*, no. 15 (May 1936): 100 p.: introduction and translation by L. Van den Bossche, 9–20: various selections.
- A Spanish edition reunites the Marian part of the two books under the title Miguel de San Augustin, *Maria de Santa Teresa. La Vida de Union con Maria*, collection Nebli: *Clasicos de Espiritualidad*, no. 11 (Rialp, 1957): 212. Présentation de Otger Steggink, O. Carm, 7–31, with bibliographical notes, 32–33, commentary on the fourteen chapters of Michel de Saint Augustin, *La Vida Maria-Forme*, 35–85; and Maria de Santa Teresa: *Textos Sobre la Union Mistica con Maria Santisima*: 3 chapters, 87–201: this is a repeat of the French edition, *Cahiers de la Vierge*, 1966, with the same subtitles. According to Father Elisée de la Nativité, OCD (*La Vie Mariale au Carmel*, in *Maria 2*, 833–961) these are the most beautiful Marian pages in the *Annales du Carmel* from the seventeenth century (p. 856). He suggests that this treatise could have influenced Grignion de Montfort. This hypothesis is interesting, but he recognizes that no proof has been found. Father Pierre H. Eckler, Montfort Fathers, who, in a remarkable mimeographed study, has restored the library of Louis Grignion de Montfort and his note-book, identifies 26 sources, in copying some passages; Miguel de San Augustin and Marie de Sainte Thérèse are not included. On the other hand, his ascetic way of consecrating himself to Mary, his missionary perspective on a level with the popular religion, differs from the Carmelite mystic way, which cultivated and analyzed the experience of the Mariform life in a more introspective way. According to O. Steggink (one of the Spanish editors), the book by Michel de Saint Augustin, which was a great success, caused the Jansenists to respond, resulting in the publication of *Salutary Advice from the Virgin Mary to her Indiscreet Devotees*, Ghent, 1673. In fact, we have no evidence of what the reaction was to this mystical writing. It is only through error and slander that *Salutary Advice* was considered to be the work of a Jansenist plot. The monograph by Father Hoffer (future Superior General of the Marianists, *On Jansenism*, Paris, Cerf, 1938) clearly shows that the Jansenists are unconnected with

this 16-page pamphlet that provoked so much controversy. It does not contain any reference to Michel de Saint Augustin or to his directee, as mentioned by Father Hoffer, nor is there any reference in his substantial bibliography (p. 369–99), nor in the index of names listed (p. 400–405).

31. 2 vol., Ghent, 1682–83.

32. Marie de Saint Therese, *Traité de la Vie Mariforme*, part 2, chap. 215, in *Études Carmélitaines* 16 (1931): 238.

33. Ibid.

34. *L'Union Mystique à Marie* (1936): 8–19.

35. *Études Carmélitaines* (1935): 236.

36. *L'Union* (1936), 28.

37. Part 3, chap. 13 in *Études Carmélitaines* 17 (1932): 289–90.

38. *Présence Mariale et Saint Jean Eudes dans Notre Vie*, no. 42 (November/December 1954): 196–205.

39. *Annales*, mimeographed edition, t. 1, p. 385, Chesnay, 204.

40. Julien Martin, *Vie du Père Jean Eudes*, Caen edition (1880), t. 2, pp. 409, 414, etc.

41. Quoted by E. Georges, CMJ, *Saint Jean Eudes* (Paris: Lethielleux, 1946), 75.

42. Letter 17, written in Tours, to Dom Raymond de St Bernard. *Correspondance*, 42–43.

43. Communicated in 1654, 13th state of prayer, article 64, in *Marie de l'Incarnation, Écrits Spirituels et Historiques* (Dom Claude Marin, reissued by Dom A. Jamet, Solesmes, 1930), t. 2, pp. 440–42, abbreviated by Dom Guy-Marie Oury, *Marie de l'Incarnation* (1976), 118–19.

44. Commentary on the same episode: Dom Claude Martin, *La Vie de Marie de l'Incarnation*, 1677, edited by Solesmes (1981), 594; cf. *Correspondance*, letter 153 from Québec to her son, October 26 1653, 521 where Marie de l'Incarnation summarizes her experience: "The presence and assistance of the Holy Virgin accompanying the soul in an extraordinary way."

45. L. Gauthey, *Vie et Oeuvres de Sainte Marguerite Marie* (Paray, 1915), t. 2, p. 31, no. 6.

46. Ibid., p. 46, no. 22.

47. Ibid., p. 53, no. 32.

48. Ibid., p. 46, no. 22.

49. Ibid., p. 75, no. 60.

50. *Letter to M. Singlin* in *Mémoires pour Servir à l'Histoire de Port Royal* (Utrecht, 1942), t. 3, p. 471.

51. No. 15, *Oeuvres*, Éd. Seuil, 447–48.

52. Ibid., no. 52, p. 465.

53. Ibid., no. 53, p. 466.

54. In *Luke 2*, no. 26, PL 15, 1642.

55. *Corona Stellarum Duodecim*, 478–79.

56. J. E. Rottner, *Paroenesis Mariana, id est Allocutiones...* (Ratisbonne 1721), no. 1015 and 1021.

57. *Annus Marianus* (Augustae Vindelicorum 1746), 315, distinctio 3, no. 2 (Redemptorist Library at Dreux).

58. Text of 1767, H. Monier-Vinard, *Le Père de Clorivière d'Après ses Notes Intimes de 1763–1772* (Paris: Spes, 1935), I, 2, p. 223–24; A. Rayez in *Maria 3*, 314.

59. Monnier-Vinard, op. cit., 1, p. 334; *Maria 3*, 315n10.

60. Ibid., t. 2, p. 49, *Maria 3*, 315.

61. Paris 1785, p. 515.

62. Note taken by Mgr. Laugeay, at Chaminade's fourth conference, *Retreat of 1824*, third notebook, p. 529, Ed. Retraites, 299.

63. *La Vie d'Union à Marie* (Paris, 1954), 252.

64. *Retraites* (1824), 299 and *L'Esprit de Notre Fondation* t. 1, p. 171, quoted by Neubert, *VS* (1937), 19.

65. *Écrits Marials* (1966), vol. 1, p. 260, no. 698; and *Écrits d'Oraison* (1969), p. 258, no. 194.

66. *Écrits Marials* (1966), vol. 1, p. 298, no. 816–18.

67. P. 159, quoted by F. M. Ragazzini, 214.

68. Text quoted by P. Bordarampé, *Le Vénérable L. E. Cestac, sa Vie, son Oeuvre* (Paris: Gigord, 1925), 458.

69. Quoted in Marie-André, *Les Visites de la Sainte Vierge à la France au XIXe Siècle* (Lefranc, 1953), 316.

70. *Derniers Entretiens*, 1, p. 253.

71. J. J. Navatel, *Soeur Marie Colette du Sacré Coeur, Religieuse Clarisse de Besançon, d'Après ses Notes Spirituelles* (Paris: Gigord, 1921), 290–91.

72. Ibid., 208; Neubert in *VS* (1937), 18.

73. Auguste Poulain, *Journal Spirituel de Lucie-Christine* (Paris, 1916); Neubert, *VS*, 26.

74. *Autobiographie*, revised by N. Pérez (Valladolid, 1929), 102, quoted by F. M. Ragazzini, 217.

75. Ibid., 162–63.

76. *Ein Leben des Lichtes: Maria Bonaventura Fink*, by a sister of the Schools of Notre-Dame (Paderborn, 1932), quoted by Ragazzini, 217–18.

77. O. Jacobs, *Dom Edoardo Poppe*, Italian translation (Milan, 1952).

78. F. Franzi, *Un Sacerdote di Maria, Can Silvio Gallotti* (Alessandria, 1952), 179.

79. Ibid., 180.

80. *Autobiografia di Madre Maria di S. Cecilia di Roma* (Turin, 1948), 87; S. Ragazzini, 219.

81. Text quoted by M. J. Nicolas, *Le Père Vayssière, une Vie Spirituelle* 22 (April 1941): 280.

82. Ibid., 280.

83. Ibid., 281.

84. Ibid., 284.

85. Ibid., 279.

86. Ibid.

87. *Sint Unum*, no. 9 (April 1953): 316–17.

88. A. Rossetti, *Con la Madonna: Vita del P. A. Treves* (Roma, 1948), 100–101.

89. Ibid., 196–98.

90. Ibid., 200; Ragazzini, 219–20.

91. E. Neubert, *Un Prêtre de Marie, le Père J. Shellhorn* (Paris, 1948), 144.

92. Ibid., 159.

93. E. Neubert, *La Vie d'Union à Marie* (1954), 270–71.

94. Alda Marcel, *De Marie à la Trinité: Frère Léonard, Vie et Doctrine* (Rodez 1952), 312.

95. This echoes the words of Chaminade.

96. *Sint Unum* (January 1954), 344.

97. In *La Vie Spirituelle* 50 (1937): 15–29.

98. (Paris: Alsatia, 1954), 328.

99. H. Lefranc in *Sint Unum*, no. 9 (April 1953): 311.

100. Réginald Garrigou-Lagrange, *La Mère du Sauveur et Notre Vie Intérieure* (Paris: Cerf, 1948).

101. Thomas Aquinas, *Summa Theologica* I–2 q. 28 a 1 and 2.

102. "*La Douce Présence de la Vierge Marie,*" *Journal de la Grotte* (April 1950), quoted by H. Lefranc in *Sint unum*, no. 9 (April 1953): 306.

103. *Journal de la Grotte* 110, no. 16 (1961).

104. *Ce que Croyait Bernadette* (Paris: Mame, 1973), 103–8.

105. R. Laurentin, *Logia de Bernadette* (Paris, 1971), t. 3, p. 40, no. 654–55.

106. "Présence mariale," *Sint Unum*, no. 9 (April 1953): 310.

107. "Présence mariale," in his Congregation's *Bulletin Sint Unum*, no. 9 (April 1953): 303–18; and no. 10 (1954): 341–52.

108. Ibid., 312.

109. *Maria, Vita Dell Anima. Itinerario Mariano alla SS Trinita* (Roma, 1966), 686.

110. G. Philips, in *Ephemerides Théologiae Lovanienses* 39 (1960): 723–24; and F. Sébastian, in *Ephemerides Mariologicae* 11 (1961): 222.

111. S. de Fiores, *Maria, Presenza Viva nel Popolo di Dio* (Rome: Edizioni Montfortane, 1980).

CHAPTER V

1. Summa Theologica II–IIqa ad2 and I–II q13, a1: *Actus fidei non terminatur ad enuntiabile sed ad rem.*

LIST OF RELEVANT PASSAGES

1. Origen (ca. 185–ca. 254): *Hom. XI in Lucam*, 1822, p. 13.

"It is inconceivable that in three months, in the presence of the Mother of the Lord and the Savior himself, Elizabeth and John did not make progress by being so close to the Mother of God and by the presence of the Savior himself."

2. Ephrem the Syrian (saint, 373): *Predicationes ad Deiparam, Predicatio Tertia*, in D. Casagrande, *Enchiridion Marianum Biblicum Patristicum*, Rome, *"Cor Unum,"* 1974, quoted by Pizzarelli, p. 78.

"You, Our Lady, Virgin and Mother, take care of me through the purity of your divine grace, guide my life and show me the way to the holy will of your Son. Give me pardon for my sins, be my refuge, protection and defense; take me by the hand and lead me to eternal life."

3. Ambrose of Milan (saint, 334–97): *Expositio in Lucam*, II, 7 and 26, PL 15, 1635 and 1642, in SC 56, p. 83–84.

"But you also, blessed mother, have heard and believed, because every soul that believes, conceives and begets the Word of God and recognizes his works. That Mary's soul may live in all to glorify the Lord; that Mary's soul may live in all to exult in God. Although there is only one bodily Mother of Christ, through faith Christ is the fruit of all of us: for every soul receives the Word of God, provided that, without blemish and protected from all vices, it keeps it chaste in matchless purity."

4. Severian of Gabala (saint, ca. 408): *Homélie sur la Création du Monde*, 10, PG 56, 498, quoted by Pizzarelli, p. 79.

"And what is prayer for, one might argue, if she does not hear? But of course she hears because she is in a beautiful place, because she is in the land of the living, she is the mother of salvation, the source of light."

"In motherhood you have kept your virginity and in your Dormition you did not abandon the world, O Theotokos. You have passed on to life, being the Mother of Life, and by your intercession you free our souls from death" (in *Minea o Libro Dei Mesi*, Rome, 1888–1901, t. 6, p. 411, quoted by Pizzarelli, p. 80).

5. Chromatius of Aquileia (fifth century): Sermon 30, 1, in SC 164, p. 134.

"We cannot talk about the Church without including Mary, the Mother of the Lord, along with his brothers."

6. Ildefonsus of Toledo (saint, ca. 605–67): *De Virginitate Perpetua Sanctae Mariae*, 12, in PL 96, chap. 12; and *Santos Padres Españoles* (ed. J. C. Ruiz), BAC 320, pp. 147–52.

"How quickly I aspire to enslave myself to this Lady, how faithfully I relish the yoke of bondage, how I want to be fully in her service, how ardently I ask never to be separated from her power!

"But now I come to you, my sole Virgin and Mother of God; I fall on my knees before you, who alone bore the Incarnation of my God; I humble myself before you, who alone has been called the mother of my Lord; I pray to you, the only one to be called handmaid of your Son, that you wipe out the punishment due for my sins; grant that I may be purified of the evil of my actions, make me love the glory of your virginity...reveal the great sweetness of your Son."

7. John of Thessalonica (seventh century): *Dormitio Beatae Mariae Virginis*, in S. Alvarez Campos, *Corpus Marianum Patristicum* (Burgos, 1979), vol. 4, no. 2, p. 463, quoted by Pizzarelli, p. 80.

"The light of her lamp filled the whole earth, and shall not be quenched until the end of time, so that all those who want to be saved receive confidence from her."

8. Germanus of Constantinople (635–733): *Sermo* 1, in *Dorm.*, III, PG 98, 344 D.

"As you dwelt bodily with those of the past, so you live with us in spirit; the powerful protection with which you cover us is a sign of your presence among us."

Germanus addresses Mary thus:

"You watch over all, O Mother of God, and your attention is on each one of us. If our eyes cannot see you, nevertheless, you live in the midst of us, a presence of love....O Mother of God, we believe that you are working in our midst." (Quoted by Albert Valensin, in *Initiations aux Exercices Spirituels*, pp. 464–65).

9. Andrew of Crete (saint, ca. 740): Oratio XIV in *Dormitio B. V. Mariae*, in *Enchiridion Marianum*, p. 1558.

"As you lived among human vicissitudes, you dwelt on a small tract of land: but since you have been transferred from this earth, you fill the whole world, as a sign of universal atonement."

10. Anonymous Author from the seventh and eighth centuries: quoted by J. B. Pitra, *Analecta Sacra Spicilegio Solesmensi Parata*, t. 1, pp. 526–27, quoted by Pizzarelli, p. 81.

"Although you have left the world, yet the whole world possesses you: everywhere signs of your presence can be seen. No place is deprived of your protection, O glory of believers, O Virgin among mothers."

11. John Damascene (saint, 700–749): Homily on the Assumption, PG 96, col. 752.

"Let us then make our memory serve as a storehouse for the Virgin....Mary will frequently visit her servants bringing all blessings with her, Christ her Son, the King and Lord who reigns in our hearts."

"Who is sweeter than the Mother of God? She captivates my mind, she delights all my talk, she is with me day and night."

12. Alcuin (died 804): *Inscriptiones*, LXXXVI, PL 101, 749.

"Even you, sweet Virgin, look with your customary kindness on your servants, who invoke you in this place. Be ever present with clemency in our prayers and guide our days always with your prayers and everywhere and keep us in the grace of Jesus Christ."

13. Theodore the Studite (died 826): *Laudatio in Dormitio S. D. Nostrae Deiparae*, PG 99, 721.

"High on her flight to the heights of heaven, Mary, the pure white dove continues to protect our earth beneath; although her body was removed, she stays with us in spirit."

14. Rabanus Maurus (blessed, ca. 776–856): *Carmina*, LXXXVII (13–14), PL 112, 1637.

"Virgin Mary, inviolate mother of the Almighty, you who are present in this place, give help to your servants."

15. Milo of Saint Amand (died 871): *De sobrietate*, II (49–52), in H. Barré, *Prières anciennes...*, p. 229.

"You, my protector, my queen, my helper, help me, I pray you, glory of noble virginity. Life whose author was born of you, by you was filled with humility."

16. George of Nicomedia (died 880): Sermon 8 in *Stabant Autem*, PG 100, 1476.

"Through John I also entrust to you the rest of my disciples. And as long as it pleases me that you dwell and live with them, you shall offer them your physical presence instead of mine. Be for them whatever mothers are for their children, by nature, or rather what I myself would be by my presence. And they shall be for you all that children are, that is to say obedient."

17. Radbod of Utrecht (saint, † 918): *Vita s. Radbodi*, 13, PL 132, 545–46.

"Fear not, Radbod, she said, be sure that she to whom you often address your prayers sees you. Do not disdain to be consoled by my presence, you who always remember me in your prayers to God."

18. Odilo of Cluny (saint, v. 962–1049): *Vita Sancti Odilonis*, II, 1, PL 142, 915–16.

"O most Holy Virgin, Mother of the Savior of all ages, keep me in your service and always assist me in all the circumstances of my life, O most gracious advocate."

19. Anselm of Lucca (saint, † 1086): *Oratio ad Sanctam Mariam*, in H. Barré, *Prières Anciennes*, pp. 229, 231, and 285.

"With great pain and a moaning heart I sigh before your merciful presence which permeates the entire universe, prostrate at the foot of your compassion, so that you look upon your servant with a face full of goodness. What could be happier for me than to be found worthy of the consolation of your love? Visit me often and show yourself full of goodness so that the sweetness of your kindness will keep far away all the bitterness of these deceitful times."

20. "Codex Gertrudianus" in H. Barré, *Prières Anciennes*, p. 285.

"I thank you with devotion, O Mary, because, although I am still soiled, corrupt and stained with various vices, you have deigned to help me with so much goodness and kindness when I call upon you with all my needs and concerns."

21. Peter Damian (saint, 1007–72): *Liber salutatorius*, BNF n. acq. Lat. Ms 186, ed. J. Leclercq, in *Ephem. Liturg.* 72, 1958, p. 303.
"Sweet is her memory, sweeter still is her presence."

22. Anselm of Canterbury (saint, † 1109): *Oratio ad Sanctam Mariam pro Impetrando Eius et Christi Amore*, in *L'Oeuvre de Saint Anselme de Cantorbéry*, t. 5, *Prières et Méditations* (Paris: Cerf, 1988), p. 285.
"Mary, Mary the great, greater than the blessed Marys, greatest of women, it is you, high and very great Woman, it is you that my heart wants to love, you my mouth wants to praise, you whom my spirit desires to venerate, you whom my soul loves to pray to, for it is your protection that I need all of my life."

23. Bernard of Clairvaux (saint, 1090–1153): *Sermon I Assumption*, PL 183, 415.
"If, at the words of Mary, the soul of these children, even before birth, is melted with happiness, then what about the exultation that has gripped the inhabitants of heaven to whom it was given not only to hear the voice of Mary, but to see her face and enjoy her blessed presence?...Mary's presence illuminates the entire universe, so much so that the heavenly homeland itself now shines with a brighter luster, in the radiance of the lamp that is the Virgin."

24. Odo of Morimond (1161): quoted by R. Laurentin, *Une Année de Grâce avec Marie* (Paris: Fayard, 1987).

25. Roman liturgy of the thirteenth century: Hymn *Veni Praecelsa*, Liturgy of the Visitation, May 31, *Office of Readings, Hymnal* (Solesmes, 1988), p. 316.
"Mary, visit us, you who once brought so much joy to your kinswoman's house. Come, bring help to the world,

remove the stains of sin, and by visiting your people, take away the risk of punishment!...Come to visit us, we pray, strengthen our resolve with a holy impulse and keep our soul from faltering!"

26. Francis of Assisi (saint, 1182–1226): Thomas of Celano, *Vita Seconda*, chap. 150, in *Fonti Francescane*, 786, ed. Messaggero (Padua, 1980), p. 711.

"Francis invented for her words of praise, offered up prayers to her, and consecrated the impulses of his heart to her: no human tongue can say how often and with what fervor he prayed. But we have good reason to be happy because he wanted to choose her as the patroness of the Order and put the brothers, whom he himself should leave one day, under her wing, that she would look after them and protect them until the end."

27. Anthony of Padua (saint, 1195–1231): *Sermone 3 per la Lode alla Vergine, Opera I*, p. 163, 6–7. [See citation p. 119.]

28. Thomas Aquinas (saint, 1225–74): Summa Theologica Ia, IIae, q. 28, a. 1 et 2, quoted by R. Garrigou-Lagrange, *La Mère du Sauveur et Notre Vie Intérieure* (Paris: Cerf, 1948), p. 254.

"Love, as Dionysius says, is an intuitive strength. There are two possible unions between those who love each other:

1. A real union when they are actually present to each other (like two people who are in the same place and who can see each other nearby).

2. An affective union (as that between two people who are, physically, widely separated from each other); this comes from knowledge (the actual memory of a loved one) and love for that person....love is enough to formally constitute the emotional union, and leads to desire of the actual union."

29. Jean Gerson (1363–1429): *Sermo de Spiritu Sancto*, in *J. Gersonis Opera* (Paris, 1606), t. II, col. 775, quoted by Fr. Girard, *Vie d'Union à Marie*, p. 180.

"O Blessed Virgin, dare we say that you are here in this temple by a real presence like your son Emmanuel?... Yes, You are here. It may not be in a bodily dimension, although a glorious body, by the privilege of its agility, can be invisibly here, yet at least you are present in this sanctuary through your spiritual influence, that you deign to exercise over those whom you love and those sweet looks your eyes bestow on us."

30. Jean-Jacque Olier (1608–57): quoted by M. de Bretonvilliers, in *L'Esprit de M. Olier*, t. I, 1, IX, *Dévotion de M. Olier à la Très Sainte Vierge*, pp. 369–39; and E. Neubert, *"L'Union Mystique à la Sainte Vierge,"* in *La Vie Spirituelle* 50 (1937): p. 26.

"One Saturday...Mary became interiorly present in my soul...She reminded me that her beloved Son had said he would only live in me through her and in her, and that the life that he lived in her would be as if she were a sacrament by which she wished to communicate her life to me."

M. de Bretonvilliers, *L'Esprit de M. Olier*, t. I, 1, IX, *Dévotion de M. Olier à la Très Sainte Vierge*, p. 409.

"He seemed to be nothing more than the same thing as the Blessed Virgin, who was more present within him, so to speak, as though he were not himself. He saw himself again confirmed in her, in a fuller participation of her grace, her perfections, her virtues and her life, and more than ever he forgot himself."

31. Michel de Saint-Augustin (Carmelite, 1621–84): *Introduction à la Vie Intérieure*, appendix to book iv, "*De la Vie de Marie-forme et Mariale en Marie à Cause de Marie*," French ed. and notes by Br. Romero de Lima Gouvea, O. Carm, Parole et Silence, coll. "Grands Carmes" (2005), pp. 570–612.

32. Marie de Sainte-Therese (1623–77): *L'Union Mystique à Marie*, in *Les Cahiers de la Vierge* (May 1936), p. 55–66, quoted by R. Garrigou-Lagrange, *La Mère du Sauveur et Notre Vie Intérieure* (Paris: Cerf, 1948), pp. 332–33.

"This sweet Mother...took me under her motherly guidance and leadership, like the schoolteacher who guides the hand of the child to teach him to write...She remains almost without interruption in front of my soul, attracting me in such a kind and motherly way, smiling at me, challenging me, leading me and teaching me in the path of the spirit and the practice of the perfection of virtues. And so I did not lose for a single moment the taste of her presence next to that of God....God reveals himself in Mary and through her like in a mirror."

And again (ibid., pp. 67, 75):

"The maternal love and favor of this sweet Mother for us, manifest themselves so vividly and clearly that there can be no ulterior motive about it, nor the slightest hint of illusion or any mixture of feelings of the natural order....My gaze remains constantly fixed on her so that in all things I do what pleases her most and what she wants. She also deigns to show me clearly, to make me understand and know what she wants in any given circumstance, whether to do something or not to do it. I would find it virtually impossible to do otherwise, because she remains almost without interruption in front of my soul....And so I do not lose for an instant the taste of her presence beside that of God."

Then (ibid., p. 72):

"It is not possible for me to make myself better understood in words, nor to say how I feel possessed by, guided by and living in Mary's spirit. And I cannot express in words how I receive in my soul the divine influx of her spirit and live through her spirit."

33. Marie de l'Incarnation (saint, 1599–1672): quoted by P. Renaudin, in *Marie de l'Incarnation* (Paris: Aubier, 1942), pp. 150–51.

"I felt her help in a very extraordinary way, which was that she was continually present to me. I did not see her with my bodily eyes, but in a way in which the most adorable Trinity did me the honor and mercy of contacting me through their union, love, and real and constant communication, which I had only experienced through the Blessed Virgin on this occasion, though I still would have a great devotion for her....But here also the union that I had with her in my heart, allowed me to speak to her through loving activity that was very simple and intense in the depth of my soul, as though to her beloved Son; I felt her there without seeing her near me, accompanying me throughout the comings and goings that were required for the building work, since we had begun to break down hovels with the aim of finishing the work."

34. Margaret-Mary Alacoque (saint, 1647–90): quoted by Henri Lefranc, *Sint Unum* 9 (1953): p. 316.

"She [Mary] made herself so much mistress of my heart, that taking me for her own, she ruled me....Since I was only young I did not dare to address myself to her Son, but always to her. The Blessed Virgin rewarded me with her presence, embraced me warmly and told me: "My dear daughter, you still have a long road to travel."

35. Arnauld (Marie-Claire): *Lettre à Monseigneur Singlin,* in *Mémoires pour Servir à l'Histoire de Port-Royal* (Utrecht, 1942), vol. 3, p. 471, quoted by A. Pizzarelli, op. cit., p. 105.

"[Mary]...The only way in which I can expect God's mercy....Most of my time is taken up with her and I cannot live except under her shadow."

36. Louis-Marie Grignion de Montfort (saint, 1673–1716): *The Secret of Mary,* nos. 54, 55, 57 (Tourcoing: Les Traditions Françaises, 1949).

"Let us set to work, then, dear soul, through perseverance in the living of this devotion, in order that Mary's soul may glorify the Lord in us and her spirit be within us to rejoice in God her Saviour (Luke 1:46). These are the words of St. Ambrose...

"This devotion faithfully practiced produces countless happy effects in the soul. The most important of them is that it establishes, even here on earth, Mary's life in the soul, so that it is no longer the soul that lives, but Mary who lives in it. In a manner of speaking, Mary's soul becomes identified with the soul of her servant. Indeed when by an unspeakable but real grace Mary most holy becomes Queen of a soul, she works untold wonders in it. She is a great wonder-worker especially in the interior of souls. She works there in secret, unsuspected by the soul, as knowledge of it might destroy the beauty of her work.

"To sum up, Mary becomes all things for the soul that wishes to serve Jesus Christ. She enlightens its mind with her pure faith. She deepens its heart with her humility. She enlarges and inflames its heart with her charity, makes it pure with her purity, makes it noble and great through her motherly care. But why dwell any longer on this? Experience alone will teach us the wonders wrought by Mary in the soul, wonders so great that the wise and the proud, and even a great number of devout people find it hard to credit them."

37. Clorivière (Peter-Joseph de, 1735–1820): quoted by André Ravez, in *Maria*, t. 3 (Paris: Beauchesne, 1954), pp. 314–15.

In 1767: "Toward the end of my prayer, it seemed to me that those words were said to me inwardly, as from Our Lady: Go your way under my protection. If I accompany you, you will reach the end. At that moment I was filled with the sweet feeling of her presence. I begged, since it had pleased her to receive me as a son, that she make me well worthy of the name, protesting that I wanted nothing more than to become a vivid image of her and her Son, suffering, despised and crucified." (p. 314)

In 1771: "What state would I die in? Saved from hell through the merits of Jesus Christ, preserved from Purgatory by the intercession and very special protection of Mary.

"The presence of Jesus and Mary, the sweet conversations I had with them in my mind, in my heart, in the center of my soul, it is that that I now hope to find." (p. 315)

"Then I received a favor from the Blessed Virgin, whose hands I kissed with great devotion and tears, but in a very spiritual way." (p. 315)

"Sometimes Our Lord and Our Lady present themselves to my soul in a sensitive way; when I talk with them with confidence and I know what they tell me." (p. 315)

Quoted by P. Monier-Vinard, *Pierre de Clorivière, d'Après ses Notes Intimes de 1763 à 1773* (Paris: Spes, 1935), t. 1, p. 334:

"After supper, having said the rosary and being more composed than usual, it seemed that Our Lady was present although invisible, which made me send her my prayers with unusual fervor....It seemed to me that Our Lady adopted me as one of her children and gave me her blessing."

38. Chaminade (G–J): *Retraite de 1824*, notes by M. Laugeay, 3rd notebook, Marianist Archives, Rome, p. 529.

"There are some who have the gift of the presence of Jesus Christ and the Virgin Mary, but this is very rare. One has to be very faithful to deserve it."

In 1824, notes by M. Laugeay, quoted in *L'Esprit de Notre Fondation* (Society of Mary), t. 1, p. 171:

"The Blessed Virgin is not among us in the same way that Our Lord Jesus Christ is."

39. Cestac (L.-Ed., 1801–68): quoted by P. Bordarrampé, *Le Vénérable L. Cestac, sa Vie, son Oeuvre* (Paris: De Gigord, 1925), p. 458.

"No, I do not see her, but I sense her presence, like a horse senses the hand of a rider who guides it."

40. Faguette (Estelle, died 1876): quoted by Marie-André, *Les Visites de la Sainte Vierge à la France au XIXe Siècle.*

"Fear nothing, you know well that you are my child...I will be invisibly close to you..."

41. Thérèse of the Child Jesus (saint, 1873–97): *Déposition de Mère Agnès de Jésus au Procès Apostolique, Summarium* (1889), p. 792, quoted by François de Sainte-Marie, in VIIIe *Congrès Marial National, La Maternité Spirituelle* (Paris: Lethielleux, 1962), p. 132.

"I was entirely hidden under the veil of the Holy Virgin...I was no longer on earth. I did everything I had to do, all my work in the refectory, as if someone had lent me a body...it is very difficult to explain, it is a supernatural state that God alone can give and which is sufficient to detach the soul forever from the earth."

42. Marie-Colette of the Sacred Heart (1857–1905): quoted by J. J. Navatel, *Marie-Colette du Sacré-Coeur, Religieuse Clarisse du Monastère de Besançon, d'Après ses Notes Spirituelles*, 1859–1905, (Paris: De Gigord), p. 208.

"It now seems to me that she [Mary] never leaves me. Although she is not visible, I feel her presence and protection."

pp. 290–291: "I find myself very often praying that the Blessed Virgin will deign to prepare me to receive Our Lord in Holy Communion. I am so unworthy of so great a work, and all my preparations are so little, that I am comforted that my dear Heavenly Mother wants to come to my rescue, giving me her heart sometimes and also the dispositions that she herself had. And this love I felt for our Lord in the Blessed Sacrament, and which seemed so lacking in fervor previously, is nothing more than coldness and indifference in comparison to what I now feel for Him. It seems to me that this is nothing but a small flame escaping from a narrow and poor heart, but it is a very huge fiery furnace of love that consumes me for the adorable Sacrament, which is my God himself, full of love for me which he gives me every day."

43. Christine (Lucie, 1870–1908): *Journal Spirituel* (Paris: Auguste Poulain, 1916).

p. 29: "This union has this peculiarity that the soul feels the Blessed Virgin as a bond of love between God and itself, like a divine intermediary."

p. 65: "Sometimes the soul is united especially to the Blessed Virgin, and it feels like a blessed link strengthening its union with Our Lord."

p. 139: "The Blessed Mother is the link, the intermediary, whether we feel it or not, between God and us. Jesus has allowed me to see and feel it more than I can express…"

44. Geuser (Marie-Antoinette de, nicknamed "Consummata," 1920): p. 127.

"It is as if God…has transformed me into Mary (I do not understand how this could be done, but the only word I can use to describe what has happened is "transform"). I felt as though I was participating in Mary's reign as Queen of Martyrs….It seems to me she asked me to call myself Mary of the Trinity. But that's merely a detail."

45. Neubert (E.): "The mystical union with the Holy Virgin," in *La Vie Spirituelle* 50 (1937).

p. 18: "To describe this union, mystics generally use the word 'feeling' as opposed to the word 'vision,' and this excludes any idea of an apparition."

p. 20: "The 'gift of Mary's presence': The awareness of sensing Mary, not residing in us, but acting within us by the influence of grace marked by her personal touch."

46. Vayssière (P., 1940): quoted by M. I. Nicolas, in *La Vie Spirituelle* (April 1941).

p. 278: "It is the holy Virgin who has done everything. I owe her everything, everything….It is she who forms us.

The path of filial faithfulness to Mary is to relive the very life of Jesus of Nazareth."

p. 281: "The smaller we are, the more we allow her to be our mother. The child means all the more to his mother because he is weaker and smaller....Life in Mary is the perfection of the way of childhood within the divine plan."

48. Ciney (Mutien-Marie de, died 1940): April 19, 1917.

"My Mother has come, and she is so good that she allowed me to taste her presence, and I found myself given up to a state which lasted three weeks....Suffering is one of the choicest graces; it is a kiss from Jesus. Do you remember that night when Jesus came to visit you with Mary, while this good Mother made you feel her presence? Jesus then asked if you want to suffer a little for him, and you said: Whatever you want, Jesus!"

49. Maria di Betania (1901–45): *Autobiografia Spirituale* (Florence: LEF, 1962), p. 57, quoted by A. Pizzarelli, p. 124.

"Mary made me feel her presence..."

50. Garrigou-Lagrange (Réginald): *La Mère du Sauveur et Notre Vie Intérieure* (Paris: Cerf, 1941).

pp. 252–53: "As God can use angels to instrumentally produce an effect as truly divine as a miracle, he may also use the soul of Jesus, his actions, and even Jesus' body, or Mary's soul, her actions, and her body. When God is the Savior of mankind and provides an instrumental physical source for producing grace in us, as St. Thomas also admits (IIIa, q 43, a 2,.. Q 48 to 6..; q. 62 a. 4), we are under the influence of the same physical humanity as Christ. However, she does not affect us since she is in Heaven. Similarly, if someone speaks to us through a megaphone from a distance that does not affect us directly, in which case there is only virtual contact and not quantitative contact with the instrument and the subject on which it operates; this virtual contact is similar to that of the sun which gives us light and warms us from afar.

"If the Blessed Virgin is the instrumental physical cause of the grace of a type that is subordinate to the humanity of Christ so we are also under the same physical influence, however without it affecting us differently than virtual contact. It should be noted, however, that the human soul, because it is spiritual and dominates the body is not restricted by place. From this point of view, all souls, to the extent that they live more spiritual lives and are more detached from the senses, become spiritually closer to each other as they become spiritually closer to God. So this explains the spiritual presence of the holy soul of Christ and of Mary, especially if we assume that both are instrumental physical causes of the graces we receive."

pp. 254–55: "The Blessed Virgin...would have an 'affective presence' as the person who is known and loved by those who love her, and in very different degrees of intimacy depending on the depth and strength of that love...

"This mode of presence is certain, and St. Thomas has admirably explained it in Ia IIae, q. 28, a. 1 and 2, where he wonders whether the union is the effect of love, and whether a mutual inhesion or inherence is the effect of love...

"So there is an emotional union that results from love, despite how remote people are. If Monica and Augustine, even though they were quite distant from each other, were spiritually very united, and because of that were emotionally present to each other, depending more or less on how deep or intense their affection was, how much more would a soul who lives every day in intimacy with our heavenly Mother be emotionally united to her?

"St. Thomas goes further....He shows that mutual spiritual inhesion or inherence may be an effect of love, despite the distance between people. And he distinguishes two aspects of this emotional union: 1. *Amantum est in amante*: the beloved person is within the one who loves, through the kindness which she inspires in him. 2. *Amans est in amato*: the person who loves is within the beloved, as they very powerfully and intimately welcome what makes them happy...

"The more love is selfless and strong and intimate at the same time, the more the second aspect (*amans in amato*) tends to prevail (over the first aspect: *amantum in amante*). Then the soul is more in God than God is in the soul, and there is something similar with regard to the humanity of Jesus and the Blessed Virgin.

"Finally, according to St. Thomas (ibid., s. 3), this selfless and powerful love produces the ecstasy of love... spiritual ecstasy, in which the one who loves, as it were, comes out of oneself, because one loves one's friend, as one loves oneself, and forgets oneself.

"Here we see what the intimacy of this union of love may be and that this presence is not physical, but emotional. It is true, however, that this affective union prefigures the actual union which we will enjoy in heaven, seeing first-hand the humanity of Christ and the Blessed Virgin. Here below, we have what seems like a prelude to the physical influence of the humanity of Jesus and probably of the Blessed Virgin, who sends us still greater grace and charity, which embed themselves ever more intimately in our will."

p. 334: "Many holy souls here below have, in a painful way, a deep and very invigorating intimacy with Mary, of which they do not have the opportunity to speak. For many of these souls, there is a very specific provision, an impulse to Mary, a gaze followed by her felt presence, sometimes only for a moment, like a mother who looks in at the room where her children are, to see if they are doing their homework. She then communicates ineffable piety, inspires more generous sacrifices, and a baring of oneself that enriches and allows one to enter into the depths of the *Magnificat* and also the *Stabat Mater.*"

51. Théas (Pierre-Marie): *Journal de la Grotte* (1950).

"All the devotees of Lourdes are offered the grace of intimacy with Mary. To benefit, you must first pay attention to the sweet presence of the Virgin Mary."